Ram Gopal Sanyal

The Life of the Hon'ble Rai Kristo Das Pal Bahadur

Ram Gopal Sanyal

The Life of the Hon'ble Rai Kristo Das Pal Bahadur

ISBN/EAN: 9783744692717

Printed in Europe, USA, Canada, Australia, Japan

Cover: Foto ©ninafisch / pixelio.de

More available books at **www.hansebooks.com**

THE

LIFE

OF THE

HON'BLE RAI KRISTO DAS PAL BAHADUR, C. I. E.

BY

RAM GOPAL SANYAL.

CALCUTTA:

PRINTED AND PUBLISHED BY RAM COOMAR DEY AT THE BENGALEE
PRESS, 33, NEWGHEE POOKER EAST LANE, TOLTOLLAH.

1886.

ALL RIGHTS RESERVED.

To
His Highness
Sree Mirza Ananda
Gazapaty Ray Munya
Sultan Bahadur.
VIZIANAGRAM.

May it please your Highness—

I have the honor to dedicate this book to your Highness as the humble token of my deep gratitude to you for your princely donation of Rs. 500, in aid of my undertaking. Were it not for this pecuniary help, it would have been extremely difficult for me to have brought out the book, so speedily, as I have been able to do. The Honorable Rai Kristo Das Pal Bahadur, C. I. E., spent his whole life in advocating the cause of the Princes and the People of India, and as your Highness is one of the foremost of Princes with a culture rare among them, I feel that by uniting the honoured name of your Highness with that of the great "Tribune of the people" I shall have marked the indissoluble union that subsists between the People and the Princes of this vast Empire, and the kindred sentiments by which they are animated in all their efforts to advance their country's good.

I have the honour to be,
Your Highness's,
Most obedient Servant,
RAMGOPAL SANYAL.

PREFACE.

To write the life of the Hon'ble Kristo Das Pal fully and satisfactorily is by no means an easy task. He has left nothing in the shape of notes or diary, and the sources from which the facts of his early and domestic life may be obtained are scanty. The same difficulty occurs, though in a less degree, in regard to the events of his public career. Private letters received by him from high officials cannot be made use of for this purpose as they are all of a strictly confidential character, and as they reflect the personal, and perhaps the private opinions of men still living, and still in the service of Government.

More than two years had elapsed since the death of Baboo Kristo Das Pal, and yet not even a suggestion had been made by any one to write the biography of so eminent a man; and if abler men have not come forward, a humble friend may be excused if he undertakes a difficult task even at the risk of failure. Public encouragement was tardy at first, and far from re-assuring. Had it not been for the prompt pecuniary assistance rendered by His Honour the Lieutenant-Governor of Bengal, His Highness the Maharaja of Vizianagram, and Her Highness the Maharanee Sarnamoye, the work could not have been undertaken at all. But pecuniary assistance was not all that was needed. I stood in need of literary help and information. I gratefully acknowledge that, but for the literary help rendered me most kindly by Baboos Shumbhoo Chunder Mukerjee, Surendra Nath Banerjee, Norendra Nath Sen, and several other gentlemen, it would have been difficult for me to complete the work.

I am deeply sensible of the many imperfections which will be found in this work; but my chief aim has been to repay, in however inadequate a measure it may be, the debt of deep gratitude which I owe, in common with the rest of my countrymen, to the memory of the late Hon'ble Kristo Das Pal.

In honouring the memory of the great dead, we create those examples by which the living may profit, and which may guide the footsteps of succeeding generations in the difficult path of social and moral reform which may lie before them. Though the prophet and the saint should die, the immortal fire outlives the organ that conveyed it, and the breath of liberty is not extinguished but survives him. Thus spoke Grattan before a spell-bound audience of the Irish House of Commons. Kristo Das is dead; but his work is being continued, and his spirit still lives among his countrymen; and it is the hope that his example of moderation, sobriety and earnest enthusiasm for the public good may continue to instruct and stimulate his countrymen in all their patriotic efforts that has led me to undertake the difficult task of writing his biography. How far I have been successful in this task, how far I have described Kristo Das as he deserved to be—the undisputed leader of the transition epoch of modern Bengal, as Mr. Cotton describes him, it will be for the reader to say.

Perhaps I ought to add a word of explanation. It may be objected to my treatment that I have given undue prominence to persons living, and still more to those long since dead and gone. No one, I am sure, who feels the absence of a biographical literature in India,—no one, above all, who, with the best of us, deplores that fatal desideratum towards the creation of Indian nationality, the absence of the history of our political noviciate, the absence, in particular, of the history of the Press, which has been and is still the best expression of that noviciate; will, I am sure, judge so captiously. Indeed, I have been encouraged and assisted by men, eminent for patriotism and for their efforts in raising our people. I am confident that the generality of my countrymen, however they may regret my want of ability,—of which none can be more conscious than I am—will be glad to hear of the pioneers in Bengali political thought. For myself I was advised, and I felt, that no Biography of Kristo Das Pal could be complete without a notice of his contemporaries, and specially of the living publicist who was his earliest literary friend, who assisted weekly in the *Hindoo Patriot* during its best period—from 1866 to 1872—under his management, and who with himself constituted, in Kristo Das's own favourite expression, "the Beaumont and Fletcher of the Indian Press—," or without an account of the great man, early cut off by an inscrutible Destiny, who was the father of political thought in Bengal, who was the Gamaliel at whose feet they sat, who, in fact, moulded the career of both—I mean the late Hurish Chander Mookerjee. It is a national misfortune that we have no record of the latter's life or collection of his scattered writings.

CONTENTS.

CHAPTER I.

	Page
Origin of the Hindoo Patriot	1
How Babu Hurrish Chunder Mukerjee got the Hindoo Patriot	4
The Sepoy Mutiny, and the writing of Babu Kristo Das at the time	
Death of Babu Hurrish Chunder Mukerjee	13
Babu Shumbhoo Chunder Mukerjee's article on the death of Babu Hurrish Chunder Mukerjee	15
Extract from the *Phœnix* on the death of Hurrish Chunder Mukerjee	22
Hurrish Chunder Mukerjee's memorial	25

CHAPTER II.

How Babu Kristo Das Pal got the Hindoo Patriot	29
Pundit Ishur Chunder Vidyasagar's connection with the Hindoo Patriot	30
The History of the Trust-Deed of the Hindoo Patriot	ib.

CHAPTER III.

Genealogy of Babu Kristo Das	32
An Astrologer's prophecy on the birth of Babu Kristo Das	33
His early education	ib.
His early writings	36
Dr. Duff and Babu Kristo Das	38
Mr. Thompson and ditto	39
Babu Kristo Das's opinion on the Calcutta Review	42
His pamphlet on "Young Bengal Vindicated"	43
His marriage and domestic Life	49

CHAPTER IV.

Lord Canning and Sir John Peter Grant	52
Sir Cecil Beadon and the Orissa Famine	54
The Railway accident at Samnagore	55
His apology to the Eastern Bengal Railway Company	59
Investiture of Sir Maharaja Joteendra Mohun Tagore, K. C. S. I., C. I. E., with the title of Raja Bahadoor	60
Prohibition of the Study of Poetry in our Schools and Colleges	62

	Page
Babu Kristo Das's reply to Sir George Campbell's attack on the Hindoo Patriot	64
Review of Sir George Campbell's administration	70
Mahesh Ruth Festival	76
Doorga Pooja at Panduah	78
The Baroda Question	79
Lokenathpore Case	81
Birthday Honours	87
The Meherpore Case	89
Dr. Mahendra Lall Sircar's Science Association	92
The Chittagong Case	93
The Vernacular Press Act	94
Text-book Committee	98
Doorga Poojah Holidays	ib.
Emigration Bill	98
Babu Surendra Nath Banerjee's trial and the Contempt Case	101

Chapter V.

His Career in the British Indian Association	105
Origin of the British Indian Association	ib.
Kristo Das's appointment as Assistant Secretary to the British Indian Association	107
Memorial of the B. I. Association on the Public Work Cess Bill	110
Ditto on High Education	115

Chapter VI.

His career in the Calcutta Municipality..?	120
The Water Supply Question	122
The Municipal Market ditto	126
The Stipendiary Magistrateship	ib.
Lord Ulick Browne	127
The Calcutta Municipality Bill	131
Sir Stuart Hogg's Retirement	141
Memorial for Mr. Souttar	144
Contagious Diseases Act	147
Deficiency in the Water Supply	149

Chapter VII.

Legislative career	153
Criminal Procedure Code Amendment Bill	155
The Bengal Tenancy Bill	167

CHAPTER VIII.

	Page
His death and character	169
His Will	171

APPENDIX.

Trust-Deed of the Hindoo Patriot in Bengali	177
Ditto Translation	179
Private Letters	181
Anecdotes	182
Specimen of Hurish Chander Mukerjee's writing in 1857	187
Ditto, ditto in 1860	192
Ditto of Babu Kristo Das Pal's writings in 1858	196

ERRATA.

Cheers *for* cheer, p. 28, line 21.
Extended *for* extend, p, 40, line 16.
Meeting *for* Meetings, p. 40, line 23.
Siobb *for* Cob, p. 36, line 19.

CHAPTER I.

EARLY HISTORY OF THE HINDOO PATRIOT AND BABU HURISH CHUNDER MUKERJEE.

It was said of Adam Smith that he had done more for the prosperity of England, than the collected labours of 50 statesmen, and the remark is equally true of the great Indian whose life is the subject of the present memoir. The memory of the departed statesman reminds us of the steady process by which alone the exalted heights of Fame can be reached. To attain eminence is not the work of a day ; it is one of gradual growth. Such it was with Kristo Dass Pal. Unknown for years, he became by strenuous exertions the leader of public opinion in Bengal. His life is the history of the progress of Indian journalism. Early connected with the *Hindoo Patriot*, he conducted that newspaper, through almost every stage of its existence, until it has come to be the leading journal in this part of the country. But if Kristo Dass Pal was the making of the *Hindoo Patriot*, the *Hindoo Patriot* was, in a large measure, the means by which he rose to distinction. It would therefore not be out of place here, to narrate as briefly as possible the history of the journal, which has exercised so important an influence on the political bearing of more than one of those who were the early pioneers of our newspaper press.

When Wilkes raised the cry of " Liberty and the '

people" so long ago as 1785, he sowed the germs of an influence which was in a short time to reign supreme throughout the length and breadth of England,—an influence which has tempered all her institutions, and which is courted by every ambitious Englishman with a deference surpassing that paid by Boswell to the great hero whom he worshipped. The cry was not taken up in India at the time, but half a century later, a still small voice might have been heard calling upon the country to awake from the political inaction under which she had so long slept. But the work of educating Hindoos was a long and tedious one, and many years passed before the *Patriot* received the appreciation it manifestly deserved.

We have already dwelt upon the desirability of giving an account of the origin and development of the *Hindoo Patriot*, but we beg the readers' pardon, if in doing so, we have to advert to the life of a man who, in his own quiet way, had made for himself an ever-lasting name. At his death his mantle fell upon a ·youthful aspirant, and Kristo Dass Pal caught up the inspiration which influenced him through life, and which died with him after his successful career had been run. But to return to our original purpose.

The *Patriot* which has, for more than a quarter of a century shaped the destinies of "Young India," and now wields a vast influence over it and the Government of the country, originated in the following manner :—

One Babu Modoo Shoodon Roy of Bara Bazar who had a Press at Kalakur Street first conceived the idea of starting a newspaper, and it was from his Press that the *Hindoo Patriot* was first issued in the beginning of the year 1853. The first Editors were the three well-known brothers of the Ghose family at Simla, viz., Babus Srinath Ghose, Girish Chunder Ghose, and Khetra Chundra Ghose. Babu Sreenath Ghose was then head clerk of the Calcutta Collectorate, under Mr. Arthur Grote, who has now retired. They were assisted now and then by Babu Hurish Chunder Mukerjee, a clerk in the Military Auditor General's office (now called the Military Comptroller General's office) on a monthly salary of Rs. 100. After 3 or 4 months, the brothers Ghose gradually severed their connection with the paper, and the entire task of editing thus fell on Hurish Chunder Mookerjee. In those dark days of the pre-University period of English Education in Bengal, the native journalist had uphill work to perform. He had no constituency to support and cheer him. The European community took no interest in Indian affairs and native newspapers in English, however ably conducted, were little appreciated by the public. There were few in those days who could read English newspapers, and fewer still who could afford to pay for them. Even the better classes were apt to think, that a paper edited by a native could not be up to the mark. Hence the circulation of the *Hindoo Patriot* was confined to a few only, and received very little public support.'

The location of the office and the press in one of the back lanes of Bara Bazar, moreover stood in the way of its success.

The proprietor accordingly transferred it to a house in front of the well-known shop now situated at No. 12 Radha Bazar Street. He hoped also by this removal to one of the busiest parts of the town, to secure printing orders. But this expedient failed to produce the desired effect, and the *Hindoo Patriot* was looked upon as a bad speculation. During this period of despondency, Hurish Chunder continued, without any remuneration, to edit the paper. He regarded it as a labour of love. No pecuniary prospect was necessary to keep alive the spirit of disinterestedness that was within him.

But a crisis had arrived which threatened the very existence of the *Hindoo Patriot*. The paper did not pay; on the contrary the losses incurred were great. The proprietor impatient of an undertaking which offered no hopes of success determined, after a few months, to dispose of the press and the paper to the Editor. Hurish had suffered great inconvenience in having to come to Radha Bazar every week and staying there all night. The offer was a reasonable one and it was formally accepted. We can form but a faint idea of the joy which must have thrilled through every nerve of the great *litterateur*, as he formed his future plans. The *Hindoo Patriot* was to be his own; he could mould it as he liked! But the difficulties which beset his path were not to be easily overcome. He was a poor clerk, and the purchase of a press was far beyond his slender means. But Hurish was determined, and for once the poet was wrong when he sang :

"Oh, ever thus from childhood's hour,
I've seen my fondest hopes decay."

By dint of the strictest economy, a sum of money sufficient to meet all demands was collected, and the purchase completed. The *Hindoo Patriot* passed into new hands and Bengal, at least, has benefited by the change.

Having realized his grand object, Hurish Chunder secured the lease of a house at Bhowanipore near his own and had the press and office removed to it. The building stood on the road to Kalighat and opposite to Moulvi Habibul Hossein's mansion. The ostensible proprietor was his brother Babu Haran Chunder Mukerjee, who was appointed manager. The annual subscription was then Rs. 10 ; but even at this rate the *Hindoo Patriot* had scarcely a hundred subscribers. It consisted of two sheets of a smaller size than the paper now issued, and was published by Babu Wooma Churan Dey. But as might be easily inferred the " get up " of the paper was not very satisfactory. With the removal of the Press, however, to the neighbourhood of the late Sudder Dewany Adalut, its financial prospects became more assuring. The educated Bhowanipore public and the native gentlemen connected with the bar and the office of the Sudder Court, (who mostly resided in that neighbourhood) felt a sort of local interest and pride in the paper, and began to patronize it.

At that time there was no other English weekly in Bengal, conducted by natives, except the *Hindoo Intelligencer*, edited by Babu Kashi Prosad Ghose; and the only journals of the same kind in the other Indian Presidencies were the *Madras Rising Sun*, and the *Hindu Harbinger* of Bombay. Amongst the earliest subscribers to the *Hindoo Patriot* was the well-known Indian statesman Mr. Sashia Shastri, now Regent of Puddocotta. From the year 1853 down to the close of the year 1855, Hurish Chunder conducted his paper with great ability, and at considerable sacrifice of time and money. In 1856 the Widow-Marriage question occupied much public attention and Hurish Chunder lent his powerful pen to the advocacy of reform. But though the independence with which the *Patriot* was conducted was not exactly calculated to secure the good will of the public—particularly the Indian public who, in matters of reform, are strongly conservative—the Editor never swerved from what he considered to be his path of duty. No considerations, however important, ever led him to sell his conscience, and notwithstanding the frequent pecuniary losses he had to bear, he uniformly refused to receive outside assistance, even when voluntarily offered by friends and admirers.

There are only two instances in which we find him breaking his resolution. It is said, that on one occasion the patriotic zemindars Rajahs, Protap Chunder Singh and Ishur Chunder Singh, of Paikpara proposed to make him a grant of a comparatively large sum of money to reimburse his losses, and to enable him to improve the *Hindoo Patriot*. But nothing tempted, he declined the kind offer, thankfully yet firmly. When, however, the type showed progressive signs of decay and complaints began to pour in, that the broken type and numerous typographical errors unduly taxed the eye of the reader, he at last consented to receive the proffered aid. He knew that to maintain his own self-respect, as well as the independence of his paper, he must rely upon personal resources and his own high character. He valued his independence and honour more than anything else. That he was a man of the highest character and rare courage, is attested to, by his colleagues still living, among whom stands first Babu Sumbhoo Chunder Mukerjee, Editor of the *Reis and Rayyat*. As a journalist he published what he thought proper without regard to popularity or interest. Babu Hurish Chunder Mukerjee never courted the favour of any body, nor did he rely upon out-side help of any description in conducting the *Patriot*, a journal the like of which can scarcely be now seen in any part of India. To notice with any approach to minuteness all his writings scattered about in the *Hindoo Patriot*, (even if the earliest files could be found), or to criticize them minutely, is impossible within the narrow compass at our command. We shall refer only to some important contributions of the great Brahmin publicist. Early in 1854 appeared a learned and philosophical article on "Hindu and European civilization—a contrast," in which he discriminated the difference between the two, proved the weak points of Europeans and defended his countrymen from the reproach of semi-barbarism. The article could not fail to attract notice, and was answered in the Anglo-Indian Press, but indifferently. The superiority of the *Hindu Patriot* in erudition and philosophy as well as in knowledge of the different systems was obvious. Without formally defending himself Hurish followed up with other articles on European, specially British sociology. Thus he compared English "Strikes" with Bengali Dharmaghats. Again he expressed his impression of the tendencies of the British democracy in the course of a review of the "Reasoner" periodical. His articles on Annexation were not only learned, and logical but brilliant and eloquent. With his usual single-mindedness and honesty of purpose, untempted by favour and undeterred by the frown of the "Powers that be," he attacked the policy of Lord Dalhousie. Nor did he when the occasion came, ever shrink from criticising the conduct of Sir Lawrence Peel and Sir James Colville, Chief Justices of the Supreme Court. However highly he respected these high dignitaries for their talents and private virtues, he regarded them as too much of "courtier Judges."

The outbreak of the Mutiny marked a fresh departure in the career of the *Hindoo Patriot*. It was during this time that it first asserted itself and was universally acknowledged.

Although Hurish Chunder had hitherto maintained the attitude of an honest and independent oppositionist, and indeed very frequently condemned Government views and actions, yet after the first quarter of 1857, his policy underwent a sudden change. He noticed the stirring events that followed, and the measures of Government in that connection, in the spirit of a true *Patriot*, interested in the cause of order. When the Mutinies broke out, he appeared in the strange character of a champion of British Rule and a supporter of the administration. And such he remained till order was re-established throughout the Empire. He proved a tower of strength to Lord Canning who was assailed most bitterly by the hostile Anglo-Indian Press, headed by the *Friend of India* of Serampore. He stood firmly by the Viceroy's side and ably supported his policy. It is said, that all throughout that fearful struggle, Lord Canning used to send Home, by every mail, copies of the *Patriot*, which were highly spoken of by Lord Granville in a Parliamentary debate on the subject of British policy in the East.

As is usual in this country the native public began to feel the value of a paper that had attracted the attention of so many important members of the Government; and it was, during this memorable period, that Babus Kristo Das and Shumbhoo Chunder Mukerjee first began to write for it. Hurish Chunder, with his usual keenness of observation was quick to discern their intrinsic merits, and their articles were often put in as editorial leaders. Beside the *Hindoo Patriot*, Babus Shumboo and Kristo Das who had from their school-days aspired to high literary distinction contributed to the *Citizen* newspaper edited by Mr. John Newmarch who was then an attorney of the Supreme Court. They also wrote for the *Hindoo Intelligencer*, *Phœnix*, *Hurkura*, and the *Englishman*. On the suppression of the Mutiny, when the Anglo-Indian Press headed by the *Friend of India* raised an outcry against native loyalty, Babu Kristo Das wrote a pamphlet called "Statements of Indian Fidelity" under the nom-de-plume of " A Hindu " which was published in 1859.

As the pamphlet contains copious extracts from various newspapers of the time in corroboration of his opinion that the people of India were, in the midst of the turmoil of the Mutinies, loyal to the backbone, we need only extract here the prefatory remarks of the able compiler.

" THE Mutinies and the Rebellion have been officially announced to have terminated. The present time therefore affords the best opportunity for considering the question as to what part the bulk of the people played in the great drama of 1857-58. Its solution, however, can only be attained by a scrutinous reference to the contemporary records, or in other words the newspapers and personal accounts published at the time. In this enquiry it should be clearly borne in mind that the mass of the writers on whose statements we are forced to rely, were urged by feelings the reverse of dispassionate and impartial,—feelings the most to be distrusted when their promptings are looked to as evidence for the purposes of historical research. But under this special disadvantage even, the people at large are acquitted of all connexion or alliance, reserved or open, with the insurgents, and not only acquitted but found to have done more than expected,—to have, in some cases by their well-judged neutrality, and in others by their active and spontaneous assistance, under circumstances the most depressing, saved the Empire. This, it is hoped, will be evident in the course of these pages.

It should also be stated that in the editing of these pages the writer followed no settled plan, and could not carry out his wishes from the nature of his avocations which vexatiously interfered with the progress of this work. He made the notes at random, and, believing that those, if published in a collected form, may serve a great national purpose, has arranged them in the present shape. More than half the pages were printed before the amnesty was announced, or its fruits were known, and if here and there remarks peep out inconsistent with the result of the moment, it is owing to this circumstance. The writer will however feel himself amply repaid if his labors, notwithstanding the many imperfections of which he is sensitively aware, be the means, as intended, of disabusing many of their errors who still maintain that the people did not only not aid the Government during the crisis, but were privately leagued with the insurgents, and of leading the future historian of the revolt to a true appreciation of the character of the event."

There was yet another cause which helped to enhance the reputation of the *Patriot*. The famous Indigo-Disturbances of 1860 roused the Districts of Nuddea, Jessore, and other adjoining places, and Baboo Hurish Chunder Mukerjee took up the cause of the Ryots. Peasant after peasant came to Bhowanipore for help, and Babu Hurish Chunder notwithstanding his limited means, did his utmost to relieve their distress—a better feeling was established between the peasant and his employer, and peace was finally restored.

It was during this period Babu Kristo Das wrote a pamphlet called " Relations between Indigo Planters and Ryots," containing copious extracts from the *Indian Field*, the *Hindoo Patriot* and other journals. The pamphlet has been placed at our disposal by the well-known Calcutta Barrister M.M. Ghose, Esquire. A brilliant article on " anarchy in Bengal " written by Babu Hurish Chunder in 1860, is extracted therefrom, in the Appendix of this book.

As a member of the British Indian Association Hurish Chundra not only helped it with his sound advice, but also advocated its principles in the columns of the *Hindoo Patriot* when they did not conflict with his own. He defended Act X of 1859 by which questions affecting rents were rendered subject to the jurisdiction of the Revenue Courts.

In the same year he wrote a petition on the Civil Service age question, urging upon Sir Charles Wood, then Secretary of State for India, the necessity of holding simultaneous examinations both in England and in India. The petition contended that, it was impossible for Hindoo students to leave their homes for a distant land in order to compete for entrance into the Service, and it was urged that some inducements should be held out to the youths of this country. Mr. Meredith Townsend brother-in-law of Mr. Marshman wrote in reply a virulent article in the columns of the *Friend of India*, to which a slashing answer was given in the *Patriot* by Babu Shumbhoo Chunder Mukerjee. In the year 1859 when Babu Hurish Chunder Mukerjee was attacked with cholera, the *Hindoo Patriot* was issued with the joint help of Baboos Kristo Das and Shumbhoo Chunder and Grish Chundra Ghose. Health failing Hurish who was obliged to remain at Beloor near Salkiah for change of air, till his death on the 14th June 1861, Shumbhoo acted as an assistant Editor, and Kristo Dass wrote at least an article almost every week. After the death of Babu Hurish Chunder Mukerjee, a meeting was held in his house attended by the Venerable Pundit Issur Chunder Vidyasagar, Babus Shama Churn Biswas, Grish Chunder Ghose, Annoda Prosad Banerjee, Gobindo Chunder Bose, Sumbhoo Chunder Mookerjee, Suresh Chunder Dutta, and it was then agreed that Babu Shumbhoo should continue editing the paper as before. It was Babu Sumbhoo Chunder who urged Babu Kali Prasuna Singhee to help the mother of the Babu Hurish Chunder and his widow by purchasing the good-will of the paper for Rs. 5,000, and this sum Babu Kali Prasuna Singhee paid to the bereaved family as a token of his gratitude to Babu Hurish Chunder Mukerjee. The trial of the Rev. Mr. Long by Sir Mordant Wells which created an alarming sensation at the time, led to the addition of a sheet to the *Hindoo Patriot* paper. Babu Sumbhoo Chunder remained in editorial charge of the paper for a few months only, and it was he who wrote the obituary notice of Hurish in that paper.

The following obituary notice of Babu Hurish Chunder Mukerjee is taken from the proceedings of the monthly general meeting of the British Indian Association held on the 26th July 1861.

"Scarcely had the Committee time to recover from the loss they have sustained in the death of their late Honorary Secretary (Babu Issur Chunder Sing) they have to lament an equally severe calamity which has overtaken this society by the premature death of their esteemed colleague Babu Hurish Chunder Mukerjee. Cut off in the midst of a career of active public usefulness, pursued in different spheres of public life, the death of Babu Hurish Chunder Mukerjee is justly mourned alike by all classes of the community. In August 1852 he became a member of this Association, and from that period of his connexion he was always an active member, an energetic and laborious Committee-man and an useful and ready counsellor. The Committee are glad to state that the Members of the Association have taken a deservedly prominent part in the recent public movement for the commemoration of his services of the lamented deceased."

At the same meeting the late Babu Peary Chand Mitter moved the following resolution.—

"That this meeting records its deep sense of the loss which the British Indian Association suffered by the untimely death of Babu Hurish Chunder Mukerjee, and its high appreciation of the valuable services rendered by him as a member of the Committee. His earnestness, zeal, and devotion to the interest of this society entitle his memory to the lasting gratitude of its members."

On his death the following obituary notice appeared in the issue of the *Hindoo Patriot* of the 19th June 1861.

"Hurish Chunder Mookerjee is dead. That fact is a volume. The country needs no more. A national misfortune of equal magnitude cannot be concentrated into an epigram more acceptable to the Electric Telegraph Office. If a thunder-bolt demolished the highest and most conspicuous steeple of a city rich in noble turrets and edifices, that city would be less beside itself than our countrymen are, at this moment. Indeed the event—event it is—is a thunderstroke. Of course, mournful as it is, it was fully expected. Death for the week previous was a question of hours. "It is true" to quote Bulwer on the death of Scott, " it is true that we have been long prepared for the event—it does not ·fall upon us suddenly—leaf after leaf was stripped from that noble tree before it was felled to the earth at last;" yet nevertheless we cannot join with the "Author of Eugene Aram" in expressing that "our sympathy in his decay has softened to us the sorrow for his death." No! The life and death of a man like the one we mourn are not to be judged of by the ordinary guage. Hurish's death is a public calamity, and the circumstances which might yield consolation on the death of a personal friend have no legitimate business to obtrude on the loss of a public benefactor.

Indeed that loss admits of no consolation, except perhaps that of resignation to the will of that Being who orders all things—even our seeming misfortunes—for our own good. But if misfortune be a searcher of hearts, our countrymen have never been subjected to a severer ordeal. Never was there presented to them a fitter occasion for all the uncontrolled vehemence of grief of which they are capable, for theirs is the loss of a "light" that never before was of Indian sea or land.

There may, no doubt, be some to whom our words will sound exaggerated or even meaningless. But those who are accustomed to observe in trifling incidents the parents of momentous events and in single acorns those of large forests, in the English nation the descendants of the Picts, and in the British Indian Empire the "development of resources" of the legacy of a physician's disinterestedness, will, we are sure, give Hurish his due. Inspite of

Mr. Disreali's emphatic opinion, the rise and fall of Empires *are* brought about by hog's lard and the unobstrusive, if not quite obscure *Keranee* in the Military Auditor General's Office effected a beneficent revolution in the Government, and chiefly in the people of British India which all the statesmanship of British India has, a century, been essaying in vain to accomplish. He may be said to have introduced disinterested patriotism in Asia. Laws are said to be nothing without manners, and had it not been for Hurish, the people of India might have lived a life of centuries more, under the progressive rule of Great Britain without being any wise other than the unmitigated dreamers even the Mogul Statesmen left them. The entire present demeanour, and almost all the better ideas which we now observe in the advanced section of the Indian population are the fruits of his influence. That influence has been exerted so silently, that by far the greater portion of the influenced' themselves are unconscious of having been moulded by one scarcely known to them all by name. Yet that influence is as real and, closely observed, as unmistakable as any which has been fortunate enough to enjoy a historian. Many, we are aware, attribute that influence to the forty years education of our Indian colleges.

Education no doubt is older than the late editor of the *Hindoo Patriot*, but education merely taught the youths Addison and Shakespeare. Thus far it went and no further. The youths confounded the means with the end. It was not until Hurish appeared that the end was distinctly appreciated. Less— by eternally sermonizing than by his living example, did he teach his countrymen individual and national self-respect. Firm though respectful, strong though decent, generous at all times, sometimes a partizan though scarcely ever insincere, with wit forgiving, and bold and original without ostentation, the leader of the *Hindoo Patriot* presented a spectacle never before observed east of the Ural Mountains, and weaned his countrymen from mere enervating poetry to politics and truth, and exacted for them respect from Europeans.

Hurish Chunder Mookerjee was the son of a Koolin Brahmin who was an employe in the Military Auditor General's Office. He was born about the year 1824. His father had four wives of whom Hurish's mother was the last. His mother who survives him, is the grand-daughter of an honored and wealthy gentleman of Bhowanipore, the present seat of the *Hindoo Patriot*. Hurish was born at Bhowanipore at the house of his mother's maternal grand-father.

He learnt his English Alphabet from his elder brother Baboo Haran Chunder Mookerje, the Proprietor of this paper. When seven years old he was entered into the local Union School, where he remained till his thirteenth year, when having reached the head of the School he left it. While yet a boy he became a *kerranee* in the now defunct firm of Tulluh and Company. There he remained many years till about the year 1851 he applied for and obtained a *kerraneeship* in the Military Auditor General's Office, worth Rupees 25 a month. The next year his salary was increased to Rs. 100. From that year forth his salary continued to increase nearly every year till about two months before his death it rose to Rs. 400. At the age of twelve he was married to the daughter of Baboo Gobind Chunder Banerjee at Ooterparah, and at about sixteen he had a daughter who died six days after birth. The next year he had a male child, and when it was fifteen days old his wife died. Four months after he was prevailed upon by his mother to marry again. His child by his first wife which, since the decease of its mother, was nursed by his mother, was carried off by cholera when three years old. Though Hurish left School early and did not ever after enter a place of education, he possessed an inextinguishable thirst for knowledge. He was a voracious reader.

At first his books were supplied by his mother, but when he got employment with Tulluh and Co., he devoted a portion of even his scanty earnings to the purchase of books. Soon after he joined the Military Auditor General's Office, he became a subscriber to the Calcutta Public Library. Before that time he had so improved himself as to be a frequent correspondent of the daily and weekly press of Calcutta. Dissatisfied with this position he aspired to be on the editorial staff of a newspaper. Accordingly he made acquaintance with Baboo Kashi Prasad Ghose the editor and proprietor of the defunct weekly *Hindu Intelligencer.* He for some time was the principal contributor to this paper. Gradually his zeal in behalf of the *Intelligencer* cooled down, in consequence of his growing difference of opinion with the editor who suppressed a number of his articles. About this time also a Hindoo family of literary tastes and powers in Calcutta started a weekly now defunct named the *Bengal Recorder.* Hurish readily availed himself of the opportunity to join it and relieve himself of his connection with the *Intelligencer* :—a connection which had become distasteful to him. Just at the time, the discussions preceding the renewal of the Charter of the East India Company began, the *Bengal Recorder* was given up, and with its subscribers for the nucleus the *Hindoo Patriot* was established on its ashes. The staff of the *Recorder* including Hurish, conducted the newspaper. As a pecuniary speculation the *Patriot* was a failure. The first proprietor therefore after sustaining a loss of a few thousand Rupees, at the end of three years, offered it for sale. No purchaser appearing, the paper was determined to be abolished and the press and the materials sold. Hurish who by economy had made a little money, rather than see the paper perish, at once resolved to invest it in a speculation which had proved a failure, and was not at all likely to prove anything better in his hands, supported by a hope that his exertions may at least make the *Patriot* pay its bare expenses. For himself he never meant to make a pice by his literary labors. In June 1855 he bought the *Patriot* in the name of his brother the present proprietor, and and removed the press and office to Bhòwanipore near his house. Up to the latter end of 1857 he had suffered on account of the *Patriot* a monthly loss of from Rs. 100 at the beginning to a small sum at the end. This he bore with an admirable complaisancy insomuch that not a breath of irritation escaped from his lips, and every body was under the impression that the paper was profitable. From 1858 it began to yield a trifling income, till at his death he left a respectable property.

The real history of the *Hindoo Patriot*, of its influence on the policy of the Government, and the character of the people, and of the great revolution it effected in both, is a subject for a volume. We shall avail ourselves of occasions hereafter to dwell on it, as well as on the other phases of Hurish's life and character. We have not touched upon the political and religious movements which he originated and led, nor on his private virtues."

"On Friday the 14th instant, at his residence in Bhowanipore died Hurish Chunder Mookerjee, late *Hindoo Patriot*.

For the calamity which has befallen the Hindoo nation our sincerest condolence is offered, though it will no wise mitigate the severity of the blow or deprive it of the magnitude and poignancy of a national affliction. In the prime of life, with his task only begun, not finished, the most remarkable Bengallee of the age has gone to his eternal repose, leaving no one to succeed to the inheritance of glorious usefulness to his people. We mean no disparagement to the educated sections of native society when we say that in the path struck out for himself by the deceased he stood single and alone, and had single-handed to fight the great fight to which he had consecrated himself. Well, therefore, may their grief be intensified by the sense of abandonment of their leadership by the only spirit in the circumstances of the times fit to be entrusted with it. So strangely had this race been disunited and denationalized by centuries of foreign domination, that the very name of patriotism was unknown among them, while constitutional resistance to oppression and wrong doing, on the part of those who possessed, or who usurped authority was not to be thought of, for a moment.

Hurish was the first Native who taught his countrymen the dignity of an attitude at once firm but respectful towards Government on the one hand, and the non-Official European class on the other, with both of whom they were daily brought into relations of mutual benefit and assistance. Such was the moderation of his tone, and general good sense of his writings, that they had a most wholesome influence on the counsels of Government, and commanded the admiration of all not directly interested in the perpetuation of fraud and injustice. In his hands the *Hindoo Patriot* has been the vehicle of loyalty towards a Government wisely heedful of popular opinion as reflected in its pages, and such we hope it will never cease to be.

Of his part during the Indigo Dispute there is no man of honor, who values above all things the rights of human beings before the supposed advantages of private enterprise, but will speak in unqualified praise. What Government could not or would not interfere to effect, what the whole landed aristocracy of Bengal was too frightened to attempt, was accomplished through the energy of one man acting on the willingness of the people. It is a record full of the profound truth that neither gold nor the power of fighting men can further the cause of popular belief, but the inborn capacity of the people to help themselves. Tell them they have rights which are wrongfully withheld from them, and they strive with a God-given energy of the Earth to which they belong, till they are free. It was as impossible to hold the ryot in chains after he had been told he was no man's slave, as it is impossible to hold Italy in Slavery, even though all Europe were banded for it.

Hurish Chunder Mookerjee received no education, and commenced life in indifferent circumstances. But there was stuff in the man not to be put down by the accident of poverty, and patient industry, united to intellectual capabilities of a very high order, won for him a distinguished position in the service of Government, as well as in the general society of his countrymen. His house was the resort of all who had advice or assistance to ask for, and both were given with a liberality which left him little time for his own proper avocations, and scant means of private hoarding. It will rest with the native community whom he signally served, without fee or reward, for so many years, whether his family is to be well looked after. A high caste Brahmin, his name adds one more to the list of Indian Reformers of the Brahminical tribe, who must take the lead of all other tribes in every movement of an intellectual nature.

Of course the memory of such a man cannot be allowed to pass away with the present generation, and we shall be glad to see our Native friends bestirring themselves suitably in the matter."—*The Phœnix*, June 17th 1861.

'Full sixteen years had elapsed from the death of Babu Hurish Chundra, before a definite step was taken to commemorate his memory. That so much delay was allowed to transpire in such a momentous matter was a circumstance to be regretted. The meagre way in which Hurish's memorial was at last resolved upon, will be apparent from the proceedings of a meeting held on the 15th July 1876 by the British Indian Association in which Dr. Rajendra Lall Mittra made a speech which we transcribe below.

"Most of his audience were well aware that soon after the death of their late distinguished countryman, a meeting was held in the rooms of the British Indian Association to vote a memorial in honor of the lamented deceased, and a committee was appointed to carry out the intention of the meeting. The form of the memorial was largely discussed at the meeting; and the different propositions then made were referred to the committee which was left at liberty to adopt any one of them, or any new one they thought proper which they could best carry out with the means that would be at their disposal. The feeling was strong in favour of a memorial building, and the late Babu Kali Prasana Shing, who was so honorably noted for the deep interest he took in every thing that was noble and generous, and conducive to the well-being of his countrymen, came forward with an offer to place at the disposal of the committee a plot of land, measuring two biggahs, situated on the Upper Circular Road, on the condition that the committee should build at their cost a suitable house for a Library, and for public meetings, conversaziones, and theatrical performances. The offer was accepted, plans were prepared, and a trust appointed, but the subscriptions raised proved utterly inadequate for the purpose. For the thousands who had professed high esteem and respect for the lamented deceased, very few indeed were found willing to come forward with their subscriptions. Five rupees per head from those who professed their friendship for Hurish Chunder Mookerjee would have raised a lac ; but those who were the loudest in their protestations were the most conspicuous by their abstinence from touching the subscription book. After years of toil the total sum realized barely amounted to Rs. 10500 !

The plan of erecting a house had therefore to be given up, and the land to be returned to the donor. A statue was next thought of, but no materials were available for the purpose ; Hurish had never sat to an artist for his likeness, and the late Mr. Hudson, who had seen Hurish often failed to produce a picture from memory. Scholarships, prizes, stipends and the like were next taken into consideration, but none of them commended itself to the approbation of the committee. At this time the British Indian Association was negociating for the purchase of a house, and as it did not require an entire house for its purposes, the committee thought the opportunity a good one for securing accommodation for a Library on an advantageous terms. Hurish Chundra Mookerjee was intimately associated with the British Indian Association for a long time. He had laboured for it most assiduously and for years. Early and late at daily desk-work, at weekly committee meetings, and at monthly and special general meetings, he was foremost everywhere, and identified himself in all its actions. The Association too did much to encourage him every way. It placed at his disposal for the support of his paper a vast mass of information, and the results of varied experience derived in different walks of life by some of its oldest and most influential members ; it offered him every facility for collecting facts and figures ; it enabled him to mature his views by free discussion with some of the ablest men of the country. Soon after his death, the members of the Association assisted in rescuing his dwelling house from sale under an attachment for debts incurred by him on account of some law expenses, and thereby saved his home and hearth ; and since then they had regularly paid pensions for the support of his mother and widow. On the death of his mother they defrayed the cost of her shradh. His widow still gets her pension. And it was supposed under the circumstances that a memorial for him would be most appropriate, if connected with the Association. The terms obtained were also the most favorable possible. For the sum of ten thousand rupees, the Trustees got the Association to agree to place at their disposal three rooms on the ground floor of its new house with the necessary out offices, with the reversion of the whole house in the event of the Association being dissolved, and no new one on the same principle, being formed within a year ; to keep the rooms in perfect repair at its own cost ; to defray all taxes and rates ; to present to the Library all books and pamphlets that it may receive as presents or by purchase ; to keep a clerk in attendance at the Library, free of charge ; to hold in custody the book, and effects of the Trust ; and to direct the servants of the Association, to attend to the cleanliness of the rooms. Thus the whole expense of maintaining the Library was secured, and it was thought that it was not at all likely that better terms could any where else be got. The negociations were at once closed, and this Library is the result. For the supply of newspapers the Trustees are indebted to the *Hindoo Patriot* who has promised to place at their disposal, all the paper that he purchases or gets in exchange of his paper. As the *Patriot* was originally established and raised to its high position by Hurish Chundra Mookerjee, and is intimately associated with his memory,—indeed it is the best monument that he could have left for himself—and which had been so ably and so successfully maintained by his successor (cheer) it was not apprehended that this source of supply of newspapers either from the present editor or his successor will in a hurry be cut off."

CHAPTER II.

HOW KRISTO DAS PAL GOT THE CHARGE OF THE HINDOO PATRIOT.

WELL nigh full 25 years had elapsed since Kristo Das got the editorial management of the *Hindoo Patriot,* and as the incidents bearing on the time must still be in the recollection of many of his personal friends, it is natural to expect that full and well-authenticated information should be forthcoming. But unfortunately, as it often happens, truth cannot be ascertained, and if ascertained, cannot be made known to the public ; for in honouring the dead, we are not at liberty to disclose the confidences of private life which may affect the living. Pundit Ishur Chunder Vidyasagar to whom we are much indebted for much valuable information, states that after the severance of Babu Sambhoo Chunder Mukerjea's connection with the Patriot, he requested its proprietor Babu Kali Prasana Shing to place the paper in other hands. Kali Prasana Shing who had a great regard for the venerable Pundit agreed to the proposal, and accordingly made over the *Patriot* to him, with entire control over it. The venerable Pundit, the patron of struggling merit, requested Babus Kristo Das Pal, Koilash Chunder Bose, and Nobin Kristo Bose to contribute, and conjointly to edit the paper, with the understanding that all profits, if any, should be divided *pro-rata* ; and that in case they failed to give satisfaction to the public, they would be removed. Kristo Das took charge of the paper in the last week of November 1861, and became its principal Editor, while his co-adjutors who helped him with contributions now and then gradually withdrew from the work. In this way the *Patriot* was conducted for about a year, when some of the members of the British Indian Association requested Babu Kali Prosana Shing to transfer the control of the paper from the hands of Pundit Ishur Chunder Vidyasagar tothemselves. He at first demurred to the proposal, but finally consented to make it over to a body of Trustees composed of Raja Roma Nath Tagore, Doctor Rajendra Lal Mitra, Sir Maharajah Jotindra Mohun Tagore, and Raja Pratap Chunder Shing. A Trust-Deed was drawn up after a short time in July 1862. On the death of Raja Protap Chunder Singh, Raja Degumbur Mitra was appointed in his place, and after the decease of Raja Degumbur, and Raja Roma Nath Tagore, Maharajah Narendra Kristo Bahadur and the Hon'ble Doorga Churn Law were asked to succeed them.

The office of the *Patriot* was now removed to Amherst Street, and Kristo Das was, under the Trust-stipulations, paid a fixed remuneration, as editor of the *Hindoo Patriot*. The accounts relating to the income and expenditure of the paper had to be regularly submitted to the Trustees. But subsequently, when Kristo Das by his able management of the paper had come to enjoy the confidence of the Trustees, the net profits of the *Hindoo Patriot* were allowed him for life. There is however a different version regarding the early part of Kristo Dass's connection with the *Hindoo Patriot*. It is said that from the earliest period of his connection with the paper, he enjoyed its net profits and was never a paid editor.

The income of the *Patriot* during this time was indeed very trifling. Kristo Das like Babu Hurish Chunder Mukerjee his illustrious predecessor had to suffer great inconvenience and pecuniary loss in conducting the paper. There were then not more than 250 subscribers, and it may be added that for financial reasons the extra sheet of news added to the *Patriot* by Babu Shumbhoo Chunder Mukerjee was discarded ; and the *Patriot* once more took the form it had, during the life time of Babu Hurish Chunder Mukerjee. In 1863, however, success had so far attended the career of the journal that it was found possible to enlarge it again. The *Patriot* which used to appear every Thursday morning began to be issued on Monday.

CHAPTER III

EARLY LIFE OF KRISTO DAS, HIS PARENTAGE AND EDUCATION.

In narrating the history of the early life of Kristo Das it will not be out of place to refer here, in a genealogical form to the names of his humble, but not illustrious ancestors, who had settled in Jorasanko long before Calcutta was made the Metropolis of British India. In the inscrutable ways of Providence, it often happens in this world that a good name of a worthy descendant becomes, sometimes, a passport to fame, not only to those who come after him, but also to those who had preceded him. Such was the case with the Pal family of Jorasanko. *

The ancestors of Kristo Das Pal earned their liveli-hood with decent competency by trade. Babu Ishar Chundra Pal the father of Kristo Das was in an affluent circumstance, but when Kristo Das Pal was born in April 1838, he is said to have incurred heavy pecuniary losses in trade. Ishur Chunder ear-

---

* Mooraridhur Pal.
|
Nilumber Pal.
|
Kowtuck Chunder Pal.
|
Sarup Chunder Pal.
|
Ishur Chunder Pal.
|
Kristo Das Pal.

ned Rs. 15 a month from a twist-shop belonging to Babu Shib Kristo Daw.

The house in which Kristo Das first saw the light was situated in Baranushi Ghose's Street. Ishur Chundra had two sons of whom the eldest had died, before Kristo Das was born. Kristo Das used to relate an anecdote of his birth to his friends which we have heard from the well-known Doctor Babu Kanai Lal Dey. It is said that shortly before Kristo Das was born, an astrologer came to the house and predicted that the expectant child would be the first man in Bengal, though his career in life would be soon run. To verify his prediction the astrologer assured the mother, that the child would bear a peculiar mark on his ear in the shape of a mote, or *anchuli*.

Kristo Das had that mote on his ear. His mother was therefore very fond of him, and it is also related by his well known friend Babu Prasad Das Dutta of Jorasanko that the mother sometimes pawned her ornaments to defray the expenses for the education of her child.

Kristo Das was sent to school at the age of six or seven. He learnt Bengalee in a Patsala attached to the Oriental Seminary then known as Babu Gour Mohun Addy's School. In 1848 he obtained a silver medal for his proficiency in the Vernacular. After studying there for three or four years he joined the English classes attached to that school about the latter end of 1848.

The following extract from the issue of the
5

Indian Mirror of the 23rd October 1878, the whole of which was corrected by Kristo Das himself, contains an account of his subsequent scholastic career:—

"In 1848 he joined the English branch of the same Seminary; and, here, also, his industry and capacity assisted him in achieving great success in double promotions and prizes. Always the head of the class, he evinced a strong taste for reading, which enabled him to retain his place among his class-fellows. But the English tuition at the Seminary having been found or considered by him to be unsatisfactory, and failing to induce Babu Hurray Kristo Auddy to introduce "Enfield's Speaker" in the class in which he read, he left that Institution in 1853, and became a private student under the Rev. Mr. Milne, a Minister of the Free Kirk of Scotland, whom he left after a short time, for the reason that Mr. Milne wanted to impart instruction in scarcely any other book than the Bible. About the time, Babu Kristo Das Paul joined a Club at Rutton Sircar's Garden Street called the "Literary Free Debating Club," and in concert with several members of it, induced the Rev. Mr. Morgan, the Principal of the Parental Academic Institution, now the Doveton College, to open a morning class in which Literature, Philosophy, Mathematics, History and other subjects, were taught. This class which, Babu Kristo Das Pal attended for about a couple of years, was eventually absorbed in the College Class of the Doveton

College, and was presided over, first by the Rev. Mr. Morgan, who had won the name of the "Indian Arnold," and, afterwards by George Smith, late of the *Friend of India*. When, about the year 1854, the celebrated Hindu Metropolitan College was established by Bubu Rajendra Nath Dutta of Wellington Square under the management of Captain D. L. Richardson, and Captain F. Palmer, a son of the great Prince of English Merchants in India, and with a tutorial staff, comprising such men, as Captain Harris, Editor of the *Morning Chronicle*, Mr. William Kirkpatrick, and Mr. William Masters, both of them men of great attainments, and the second of them, considered by a general consensus of opinion among the first mathematicians of his day. Babu Kristo Das Pal joined the new Institution, which at once secured so large an amount of popular favor as seriously to lessen the number of the students even at the Hindu College, backed as it was by the direct support and encouragement of the State. The care and diligence with which he prosecuted his scholastic studies at this Institution, obtained for him such a measure of success that he won scholarships for two years consecutively; and his examination papers were so much above the average, as to have merited the commendation of such strict examiners as Mr. Eglinton and Dr. Mouat. In 1857, he left College, and began to store and enrich his mind by knowledge derived from a course of reading at the Calcutta Public Library and the Library of the Metropolitan College ; and he received much assistance from the late Mr. W. Kirkpatrick in the selection of books, in the practice of English composition, and in critical study of the English language. While still a student at the Metropolitan College, Babu Kristo Das Pal began contributing to the public prints ; and his earliest writings appeared in the *Morning Chronicle*, without the knowledge of its Editor, Captain Harris, his Professor who, however, gave indirect encouragement to his literary predilection. Before this time Babu Kristo Das Paul, conjointly with Babu Shumbu Chunder Mukerji had started the *Calcutta Monthly Magazine* which was dropped after a short course of six months. The Magazine was owned by Babu Prosad Das Dutt, Proprietor of the Grant Dholket in the Saugor Islands. From 1857, he began contributing regularly to the newpapers. The Editor of the *Englishman* newspaper, Mr. William Cob Hurry valued his contributions much. On the publication of the *Central Star* at Cawnpore under the editorial management of Mr. Knight, the aeronaut, Bubu Kristo Das Paul became the Calcutta correspondent of the paper, and wrote under the *nom de plume* of " Blue Bird." His pen was next employed on the staff of the *Hindoo Intelligencer*, a paper which was edited by Babu Kashi Prasad Ghose, the Indian Poet, whose name is perpetuated in Richardson's " Selections" from the English Poets."

Babu Shumbhu Chunder Mukerji and Babu Buddon Chundra Sett of 17 Noyan Chand Dutt's Lane were his school-fellows. The former gentleman says that, Kristo Das reading in the 10th class of the Oriental Seminary held the first place in his class, and used to emulate him in acquiring the arts of composition. The rate of schooling-fees levied from the students at thetime, varied according to the circumstances of the guardians. Some used to pay Rupees three, some Rupees 2, and so on. His subsequent career at the Seminary has been sketched by Babu Buddun Chunder Sett in a letter addressed to the *Englishman* newspaper, and published in its issue of the 15th September 1884, from which the following extract is given :—

" With unequalled zeal and perseverance he prosecuted his studies in the school. Whatever work he read, he read them thoroughly. Never did he acquiesce in the views of a writer without scrutinizing them. At the age of 15, when a student of the Oriental Seminary, he joined a society styled the "*Calcutta Literary Free Debating Club*," at Rutton Sircar's Garden Street. Through his undivided exertions he raised the Association to a conspicuous position. His essays and speeches always commanded respect and attention. He sometimes spoke for about an hour on a prescribed subject. On one occasion he displayed much wit and talent in his discussion on the most important question of the day, " The Russian War." His knowledge of politics even then commanded admiration. At his request, Professor E. B. Cowell, of the Hindu College, and Mr.

William Kirkpatrick, of the Metropolitan College, delivered addresses to the Society, the former gentleman on "The History of Greece," and the latter on "Trial by Jury." In 1856, Mr. George Smith, Principal of the Doveton College, having intimated his intention of reading to the Society a discourse on "The influence of country on the formation of National Character," Babu Kristo Das on behalf of the members wrote a letter to the Rev. Alexander Duff, D. D., who had then just returned from his native country, to preside on the occasion. Myself, as Assistant Secretary of the Society, and Babu Kristo Das waited down-stairs at the residence of the Rev. Doctor to receive his reply, which was as follows :—

———Buildings,
March 5, 1856.

Dear Sirs,—It will afford me much pleasure to respond to your request. Kindly, then, let me know the time and place of the meeting that I may arrange to be present.

I rejoice in every movement calculated to awaken and direct the intelligence of the people of this land.

Discussion on important subjects conducted in point of fairness and candour, cannot fail to contribute to this desirable end.

Yours very truly,
ALEXANDER DUFF.

On the appointed evening, after Principal Smith had finished his lecture, and Dr. Duff spoken at some length on the occasion, Babu Kristo Das replied to the reverend gentleman, touching on one or two points of his statements. The audience had been surprised to observe a beardless boy thus to boldly contradict so profound a scholar and an orator as Dr. Duff. Babu Kristo Das had read and hard of the fame of Mr. George Thompson as an abolitionist and a great orator, who evinced a lively interest in the political reformation of India. On learning that he had again come to Calcutta, he with other members of the Club resorted to his residence in Park Street, and handed over to him a letter drafted by himself for the Secretary, requesting him to deliver a lecture to the Society. Mr. Thompson orally replied to the following effect :—" It was not his province here to deliver lectures in a Society as theirs, held as it was in an obscure part of the town. If they required such for their improvement, they should call on the Professors of the Doveton College, or some other educational institution, as they were the best individuals to serve them with a good literary treat. His object was to redress the political grievances of India. There was only one native in the country who understood something of politics. He was (holding up the *Hindu Patriot*, which was then on his table) Babu Hurish Chunder Mukerji, the talented editor of this paper. If they wanted to do substantial service to their country, they should carefully read Taylor's History of British India, and closely watch the proceedings of the Government every moment. Then let them inform him how and what they feel, and what they required him to do. Let them eventually call a meeting at the Town Hall, and he would gladly be at their service. Babu KristoDas was highly rejoiced to hear whatever fell from the lips of the great orator. On his way home he pronounced him to be a very able man—one with whose views he entirely agreed.

It was Babu Kristo Das who suggested to the *Calcutta Literary Free Debating Club*, that a letter conveying thanks to the British Government for the supression of the Mutiny of 1857, should be drawn up and forwarded through the British Indian Association. He himself, for the Secretary of the Club, drafted the letter. It extend to about three pages of foolscap. It was so well written that Babu Issur Chunder Singh, the then Secretary of the British Indian Association, replied to it, thanking the able suggestion, and promising to carry out the proposal without delay. Babu Kristo Das attended almost all meetings of the Club, drew up the proceedings of every special Meetings, and the Annual Reports of the Society, and had them published. These reports he circulated to almost all the editors in the town for review. His memory was so wonderful that he put up all the remarkable speeches almost *verbatim*. The way in which they had been written spoke much of his abilities. In fact he was the life and spirit of the Society. He had been to the Calcutta Literary Free

Debating Club in his early years what he was to the British Indian Association in his latter days. He visited Associations established in different parts of the town. Amongst them, the "Perseverance Society" was conspicuous. The Calcutta Literary Free Debating Club had eclipsed all of them through the noble efforts of Babu Kristo Das. Rule 14 of the Club ran thus :—" Every member is to pay one rupee and eight annas as annual subscription." Babu Kristo Das was sorry that he could not afford to pay it ; nevertheless he had been exempted from the rule as a special case, in consideration of the benefits, the Society received at his hands. Once he intimated his intention of parting from the Association, though most reluctantly, when a member spoke to him in disrespectful terms on the subject. The matter had, however, been settled to his satisfaction. The Calcutta Literary Free Debating Club had ceased to exist a few days after Babu Kristo Das had joined the British Indian Association, when he gladly gave up all his connexion with it."

"At Kansaripara, in a lane now styled after his own name, was situated the former but the humble residence of Babu Kristo Das. There, in the outer apartment, in a *khapprel* hut on a *tucktaposh* spread over with a wornout mat, where the rays of the sun peeped through the crevices of the thatched roof, he was often seen pouring over his books or writing articles for the press. The implements of his writing, on account of his humble position were indeed very inferior in quality. High and noble as his mind was from his infancy, he kept himself satisfied that they would as much serve his purpose as the best of stationery. His object was to improve, and do good to his country."...

"Kristo Das once saw me reading a certain number of the *Calcutta Review*. He observed that the perusal of such books could not render knowledge solid. He pointed out to me what books should be perused, and how they were to be read. The arguments and views of the writers had to be throughly sifted before they were taken as correct. He also added that constant intercourse with individuals of superior intelligence, position and character, was one of the best passports to one's rise and progress in the world. To see such a young lad speak in the above strain not unlike a wise man of two score years and ten was indeed a marvel. There remains little doubt, however, that by the strict adherence to these principles, Babu Kristo Das rose to so great an ascendancy."

"At the age of nine or ten, Kristo Das used to sit on a tree which stood near his old abode. His fellow comrades he addressed as his soldiers, and himself as their king or commander. Men of intelligence who perceived him thus, remarked that his features apparently bore the stamp of his future greatness."

Thus it would appear that his yearning after learning led him to Debating Clubs to take part in discussions on current political, social and religious matters. He used to feel great pleasure in hearing lectures, no matter by whom and when delivered, and he used to walk (there was no tramway in those days) even to such remote places as Bhowanipore to hear lectures delivered by his predecessor Babu Hurish Chunder Mukerjee at the Local Brahmo Somaj Hall. At an Anniversary Meeting of David Hare the "Father of English Education" in this country held at Babu Kali Prosanna Singh's house, on the 1st June 1856, presided over by Rajah Kali Kissen Bahadoor of Shova Bazar he read an essay on "Young Bengal Vendicated" which then attracted considerable public attention. It was written in such a way, that even Sir Cecil Beadon read it with great pleasure, and admiration; and it was published in a pamphlet form at the cost of the Hare Anniversary Committee of which our late distinguished countryman Babu Peary Chand Mitter was the Secretary. The work was dedicated to his great patron Babu Hurro Chunder Ghose, then a Judge of the Calcutta Small Cause Court and who used to take a fatherly interest in his education and welfare. The pamphlet has been placed at our disposal by Babu Budddon Chunder Sett. The essay after referring to the attacks that had been directed against "*Young Bengal*," went on to say:—

"However, the time is come when *Young Bengal* should be vindicated—when things regarding him should be set aright—when the breath of calumny against him should be stopped—when his just attributes should be stated in the Book of Observation and Faith. It is indeed an act of cowardice not to call things by their right names—not to represent *Young Bengal* as he is. Woe unto those, says the Christian Scripture, who call evil good, and good evil, for there is the greater damnation. Plutarch observed, that it were better that men should say, that there was such man as Plutarch, than that they would say, there was a Plutarch who used to eat his children. And should not the language of *Young Bengal* be of that strain, when he is traduced for what he is not really guilty of, when he is misrepresented and blasphemed? The poet who disfigures human nature deserves ill of the world. Byron, despite all his mighty 'energy, all the potency of his words, the brilliancy of his imagery, and the dash and spirit of his description, is little honored, because he has distorted and discolored humanity, and set down all of man in malice. And the social Byrons—those who malign men and manners—merit no better fate. The illiberal portion of the Europeans here who fall foul of us for no rational reason whatever, sin against their transcendant civilization and Christian morality by fostering in themsuch a pernicious and ill-breeding disposition.

In judging of the character of *Young Bengal* we must bear in mind, Gentlemen, ! the state of the country, some forty years ago. A Captain, on his return to England, was asked "How did he find

India ? What did he see there ?" Fortunately, no demon of Macaulay or Marshman, worked in him—he spoke all that he saw—to be brief, he breathed "the eloquence of truth." Misgovernment, answered he, rides rampant upon the land,—law is unlawfully administered—justice is unknown—plunder is the road to success—the people are grossly ignorant and blindly manacled by superstition and idolatory—their society is ill-constructed—nevertheless they are gentle and generous. Such was the language of one who visited India since some forty summers. What would he say, were he to reach the shores of England to-morrow ? Of course the times are altered —and the change in the condition of the country must make a change in the tone of his reply. Though the revolutions of the seasons have not been attended with any great revolution in the principles of our rulers, yet there has come over the country one change which the Captain had not the opportunity to observe, and which is worth chronicling. A new race has risen on the land which had ere long had no name or local habitation. The worthies of their newly-sprung up class are a glory to the nation. Their appearance marks a proud era in its history. The people of Bengal were long under the enthralment of ignorance and barbarism,—the grossest superstition governed their habits and taste. The priest had an almost absolute sway over them—before the altar they sacrificed the comforts and elegancies of life. But the new generation, strong with the armoury of Western learning, have broken down the trammels, and asserted intellectual freedom, have dethroned the Demon of false religion, and disacknowledged the prescriptive despotism of the clergy."

He thus vindicated the educated natives from the charge of denationalization.

"It is an observation generally made by the orthodox portion of our countrymen that the study of the English language has quite Anglicized *Young Bengal*. He has thoroughly become English in his habits and thoughts. His nose stinks at the sight, and his ears tingle at the sound of a thing absolutely used by the Hindus. He sees nothing good in his own society. There is with him, after all, something in a name, whatever Shakespear may say to the contrary. This is a lie. The "educated" Native has not been denationalized by imbibing English thoughts, and communing with English feelings. Yes, time was when the elder portion of the educated natives— when the Patriarchs of the new class—used to abuse and slander their countrymen, to expose, to ridicule all that smacked of "Hindooism," to look with optics which deceived them, to deal out damnation to every thing that pretended a Hindu origin. They used to extol the English to the skies, and see in the British Government the traits of All-Perfection. They used to breathe a spirit of hostility to men of their color. That hour must stand accursed in the calendar when education gave rise to such pernicious results. But thank God!—the days—the days of national detraction and contumely—are no more! A new era has dawned upon us. The stream has taken another course. The good Angel of a "*Hindoo Patriot* now works in the informed and enlightened souls of Bengal."

He thus describes the duties of *Young Bengal* "*Young Bengal* is the Reformer of the country. He it is, who with an undaunted heart of a Wallace, and with true Luthern Spirit, has besieged the citadel of old prejudices, the Sevastopole of antiquated superstition, and has, be it recorded to his glory, obtained the surrender of the greater part of the out-works and much of the interior. While the old Hindu folds up his arms, breathes a hostile breath, turns a deaf ear to all cries for the social amelioration of his sisters and daughters, and sits inexorable to all prayers for the same, Young Bengal sets forth and cordially embraces the proposal of the Philanthropists and Friends of India, and pledges to carry them out, when they lie within his stretch. Was it not the "educated" Native who co-operated with the late Honorable Mr. Bethune, and stood fast to him in his philanthropic exertions, through good and evil report? Is it not the "educated" Native who has prolonged the sacred existence of the glorious movement of Rajah Rammohun Roy—that honorable name, at the mention of which the pulse of every true Hindu beats with quick emotion, and his heart leaps with joy ? Is it not the "educated" Native who has been the most instrumental in inundating the Legislative Council with petitions from various parts of India, praying for the legalization of Widow Marriage ? Is it not the "educated" Native who has had the courage to tear the shackles which the interest of the Brahmins puts upon him in seeing foreign lands, and to sail beyond the Brahmapootra, and in the Kingdom of the golden-footed Barbarian of Burmah ? It is a needless task to hammer down on the attention of the Indian Community, that all good that has been effected in this country, has mostly proceeded from the exertions of *Young Bengal.*" We have not space for more extracts, and therefore cut short here.

On the publication of his pamphlet in 1856, a virulent article under the heading "Vanitatus Vanitatum" appeared in the *Friend of India*, from the pen of its editor, Mr. Meredith Townsend criticizing the young writer in a disparaging tone. Captain D. L. Richardson who took a deep interest in the welfare of his ex-pupil replied to Mr. Townsend's article in his own journal called the *Calcutta Literary Gazette.*

After leaving the Metropolian College, Kristo Das obtained the appointment of translator in the Court of Mr. Latour, then District Judge of Alipore. He held that appointment for a few months only, and sometime afterwards, through the influence of his great patron 'Babu Hurro Chunder Ghose he obtained the post of Assistant Secretary to the

British Indian Association in December 1858 on a monthly salary of One hundred and twenty five Rupees.

We conclude this Chapter of the history of Babu Kristo Das by noticing the chief events of his domestic life. Providence, in his mercy, showered upon him many blessings and endowed him with rare intellectual and moral gifts, but denied him the inestimable boon of domestic peace and comfort. Deep domestic afflictions, darkened in succession, the path and prospects of his life, all through.

Providential visitations overtook him year after year, and these calamities which must have shortened his life, he bore with that admirable resignation which we can expect only from men of his stamp.

At the early age of eighteen in 1856 he married Srimutty Karoonamoye Dashee, daughter of Babu Khetra Mohan Pal, of Jorasanko at the earnest request of his parents, and of his great patron Babu Hurro Chander Ghose. The parents were naturally anxious that their only child should get married, that they might have the good fortune of seeing a grand-child before their deaths. By this wife he had one daughter, still living, and three sons of whom the eldest, the sole survivor, is Babu Radha Charan Pal, the other two having died, while young, from cholera. The first wife whom he loved most dearly died on the day previous to the Saraswati Puja in the year 1872 from the dreadful disease to which her two children had already succumbed. This sad bereavement must have been a death-blow to Kristo Das Pal. Having lost his first wife he was determined not to marry again, knowing fully well that the sands of his life would soon run out. After a year or two his parents and friends again urged upon him the desirability of marrying a second time. This he did with great reluctance.

In 1874 he married the daughter of Babu Gopal Chunder Mullick of Jorasanko. Such was his reluctance in the matter that this marriage was celebrated most privately at a garden house belonging to a friend. By the second wife he had a son who died from liver complaints when scarcely two years old. What the state of the mind of Babu Kristo Das Pal was will be apparent from the few following pathetic lines written by Kristo Das himself to Mr. Lethbridge in a private note addressed to him :—

"God has smitten me sorely, and I must try to be resigned, but can feel no further interest in life ; and shall not live long."

CHAPTER IV.

HIS JOURNALISTIC CAREER.

Kristo Das as a Journalist stood first among his native contemporaries. The unrivalled success achieved in this line was due to his moderation, tact and great ability. Mr. George Smith of the *Friend of India* used to say that Kristo Das had a happy knack in the selection of subjects for editorial remarks. He knew what subjects to write upon and when. Whatever he wrote, he wrote with great insight. Though he did not make use of much rhetorical and showy language in dealing with any particular subject, yet he could discuss matters, so well backed with facts and figures that his editorials were often pronounced to be the ablest by the best Anglo-Indian writers of the day. By his moderation he won the confidence of the Government and high officials, who knowing well that Kristo Das was not the man to betray their confidence used to communicate to him secret reports of Government, and these secrets he never divulged in his life.

In the discharge of his public duties, occasions no doubt arose, when he had to criticize the actions of Government and its officials in an unpleasant tone but he was always dignified and moderate.

Sir Stuart Hogg used to say of him that at the Municipal Board when Kristo Das criticized his conduct he never took offence, but when his other colleagues found fault with him he felt greatly offended.

Within three or four months of his taking charge of the *Hindoo Patriot*, Lord Canning retired in March 1862, and Kristo Das wrote an admirable article on his administration the concluding sentences of which ran thus :—

"It is essential to our political position, to the immensity of the interest we represent, that the men who rule over us should be made known that we can appreciate the worth and testify that appreciation in a befitting manner when occasion requires. However the "colonial" party may bully and browbeat our administrators into a forced recognition of their spurious importance, the British public still look to the opinion of the people of India for a true estimate of the merits and demerits of the rulers of the country."

In April 1862, Sir John Peter Grant, the second Lieutenant Governor of Bengal retired and Kristo Das, in reviewing his career, wrote a long and able article in the issue of the *Hindoo Patriot* of the 14th April 1862 from which we extract the following :—

"To Sir John the country is indebted for many legislative and administrative reforms. It was he who, as Accountant General, set the Accounts of Bengal to order, and reduced the transactions of mufussil treasuries to manageable proportions and to a comprehensible system. As Secretary to the Government of Bengal, he was active, energetic, and for a time all-powerful. It was he who cleared the Covenanted Service of some of its rank weeds, infused vigour and activity in all departments, and gave the Uncovenanted Service a status and dignity hitherto unknown. As a Member of Council his powers found a new field for display, and we may state that there were few Members of the Administration when he was in Council, who exercised an influence half approaching to his. Whether in Finance, or in Home or Foreign politics, Mr. Grant was the *Alpha* and *Omega* of the Council."

"During the crisis of the Sepoy Mutiny he was the right hand of Viscount Canning. When the hurricane of the Mutiny first swept over the country, Lord Canning was not unnaturally thrown out of balance, and it was in that hour of temporary trepidation and panic that his Lordship opposed Mr. Colvin's conciliation policy and declared for ruthless vengeance, but guided by the wise counsels of Mr. Councillor Grant and Mr. Secretary Beadon, he regained self-possession and initiated the self-same policy of conciliation for which he had erewhile unjustly censured the late Lieutenant Governor of North Western Provinces. Many go the length of saying that Mr. Grant was the author of the celebrated Resolution of the 31st July 1857, which got the Governor General the nick-name of "Clemency Canning," but whoever the author of it, it is now undoubted that Mr. Grant's share in it was great."

A large public Meeting was held to perpetuate the memory of Mr. Grant. A committee was appointed for the purpose of which Kristo Das was Assistant Secretary.

Sir Cecil Beadon's administration though welcomed at first by Kristo Das Pal, was much criticized afterwards, during the Orissa Famine of 1866. The tocsin of alarm was first sounded by Kristo Das in the issue of the *Hindoo Patriot* of 16th October 1865 from which we quote the following lines :—

"There is already a famine raging in Orissa. It is said that rice is selling there at six seers to the rupee. So far as Orissa is concerned the Government, holding the landlord right, is under a peculiar obligation to it. On previous occasions when the calamity was by no means so severe or widespread, it did not repudiate that obligation, and we can not believe it will pursue an opposite course in the present crisis."

In subsequent issues of the *Patriot* he dwelt upon the horrible aspect of the calamity, but as is usual in this country, he failed to rouse the Government to take proper steps in the matter.

Sir Cecil Beadon in his memorable Minute on this subject, thus alluded to the part played therein by Kristo Das.

"It may suffice if I refer only to the *Englishman* and the *Hindoo Patriot*, the one being the leading English and the other leading Native Journal at the

Presidency, and to the *Friend of India*, paper published at Serampore."

"In the *Hindoo Patriot* there was no particular allusion to the famine till the 5th March (1866) when there appeared a letter from a Native Member of the Pooree Relief Committee, describing what had been done by the Committee, appealing to the public for funds. But in the article noticing the letter, though I was taunted with having told the people at Cuttuck, that no Government could do much to prevent or alleviate famine, not the faintest suggestion was offered as to how the Government could do more, for the people than it had then done by providing money for the employment of labour, by organizing measures of charitable relief. The *Hindoo Patriot* did not recur to the matter of the famine till the 2nd April."

Kristo Das pointed out the Lieutenant Governor's error quoting chapter and verse of what he had written on the subject before the 21st October 1865 when the Commissioner of Cuttuck first telegraphed to His Honour.

THE RAILWAY ACCIDENT AT SHAMNUGGUR ON THE
EASTERN BENGAL RAILWAY.

Kristo Das exercised a great deal of discretion and circumspection in writing upon subjects susceptible of contradiction. He was never hasty in jumping at a conclusion without taking pains to ascertain the real facts. The guiding principle of his journalistic career was to urge upon the authorities in as respectful and loyal a manner as was compatible with his dignity, the wants, aspirations and grievances of his countrymen. He may have carried this principle to excess on certain occasions which might be interpreted by unfriendly critics to be something savouring of adulation. It is not our business to vindicate his character here, but what we intend to lay stress upon is, that some times, in his onerous task of representing the grievances of the people he had to fall into great difficulties. One such instance occurred in the year 1868. In the month of May a terrible Railway collision took place, at the Shamnuggur Railway Station, on the Eastern Bengal Railway line. The panic among the natives residing in the suburbs of the Metropolis was great, and exaggerated accounts and wild rumours were circulated freely. Kristo Das who was not then experienced enough in his Journalistic duties was not unnaturally carried away by these exaggerations. In the issue of the *Hindoo Patriot* of the 11th May 1868, Kristo Das wrote a leading paragraph on the subject which runs as follows :—

"The down mail train came in collision with the 5-40 P. M. up-passenger train at the Samnuggur Station, and resulted in the first five or six vehicles being dragged across the ballast and turned over, the first three carriages becoming complete wrecks.

Twelve persons were killed and eight others wounded. Medical assistance was rendered on the spot, and ten passengers seriously injured were carried to the Barrackpore Hospital. The accident is attributed to the carelessness of the pointsman, who has absconded, and a warrant has been issued by the Magistrate of the 24-Pergunnahs for his apprehension. This is the official account. From the statement which have reached us we gather the number of killed and wounded must have been very large. Some estimate the killed at 100 and the wounded not fewer. We are told that the carriages were overcrowded more than ordinarily, a large number of passengers having come from the Eastern Districts for pilgrimage to Poori. An intelligent eye-witness, himself a sufferer, tells us that when he jumped down from his carriage, which was a second class one, about half an hour after the accident he saw on a rough guess more than 100 persons lying dead or half dead. All the carriages had not then been cleared, and the number must have considerably increased, since. The Railway employes made great exertions in clearing the wrecks, but in the attempt they showed little consideration for the wounded and must have, according to our informant, trodden to death several unfortunate persons who had not strength to move. It is of course now difficult to ascertain the exact number of killed and wounded, but an approximate idea may be formed by calling for the register of tickets sold for the train in question and by examining some of the more intelligent passengers on the train and the villagers in the neighbourhood, who were eye-witnesses of the scene * * * * As a matter of fact we have heard that the train was run slowly from Kanchraparah to Nyehatty, but from the last mentioned station with the usual force. Indeed it is believed that if the speed had been checked the collision would not have been so fearful, nor the results so disastrous. Again, it is strange that the break-van and three or four forward carriages passed the points in order, and the others were disrailed. Was it entirely the faults of the pointsman? May we also ask whether a goods train was run with double engine power, rather unusual, at 3 o'clock or there about in the morning of the Friday, and whether dead-bodies were carried in it ? How were the dead officially reported disposed of and by whose order ?"

In a series of articles he animadverted on the conduct of the Railway officials and the Government. The Railway Company there upon brought in the High Court Original side an action for damages laid at Rs. 5000 against the printer and publisher of the *Hindoo Patriot.*

Kristo Das finding it hopeless to corroborate his own assertions by a strong testimony of native witnesses, who were found reluctant to boldly come forward, at last had the magnanimity to make the following *amende Honourable*, to Mr. Franklin Prestage, the Agent of the Company.

Calcutta
22nd October 1868,

"Sir,—With reference to the action for libel, which the Eastern Bengal Railway Company have brought against Audhor Nath Mookerjea, Printer of the *Hindoo Patriot* in the High Court at Calcutta, in respect of an article published in such paper on the 18th May last, imputing negligence to the Company and its officers in the conveyance of passengers, and also reflecting on your conduct and that of the Company's officers in the treatment of the passengers wounded and killed in the recent accident at Samnuggur, and in the disposal of the bodies of those killed in such accident, I have through the intercession of friends informed you I am prepared to publish an apology in the *Hindoo Patriot* to be approved of by you, and to pay the costs of the action instituted by the Company.

As you have agreed to accept my proposal, I now beg to express my unqualified apologies and regret that the article in question should have been published, and I hereby withdraw all imputations against the management of the said Company, and the conduct of its officers contained in it. The article in question was written in perfect good faith, but I am now satisfied from the report of the Committee appointed by Government to enquire into the accident, that the statements complained of are inaccurate and exaggerated.

I will pay the Company's costs of the suit when taxed as between Attorney and Client under scale 2 and you are at liberty to use this letter (a copy of which will appear in the *Hindoo Patriot*) as you think proper.

        I am Sir,
       Your obedient Servant
       (Sd.) Kristo Das Pal.
       Editor Hindoo Patriot.

To
  Franklin Prestage Esqr.
   Agent Eastern Bengal Railway." *

THE INVESTITURE OF THE RAJA (NOW SIR MAHARAJAH) JOTEENDRA MOHUN TAGORE WITH THE TITTLE OF "RAJAH BAHADUR," AS A PERSONAL DISTINCTION AND THE HON'BLE KRISTO DAS PAL.

On the night of Thursday the 27th July 1871, this grand and auspicious ceremony took place at Belvedere with the usual eclat. The Hon'ble Kristo Das told us once privately, that at this time he had been suffering from the dire disease of Diabetes from which he had partially recovered through the judicious treatment of Kabiraj Romanath. He had

---

*Mr. John Cockrane the Advocate brought about a peaceful settlement of the affair and let it be said to the honour of the Railway Company that they did not take the costs from Kristo Das Pal.

then neither sufficient strength nor inclination to attend the ceremony. Yet at the urgent request of his friends he had to go to Belvedere. Sir George delivered a speech on the occasion, and as there were no newspaper reporters present the speech was not published in any of the morning papers. The speech runs thus:—

"Rajah Jotindra Mohun Tagore.

I have to convey to you the high honour which His Excellency the Viceroy as the representative of Queen Victoria has been pleased to confer upon you. I feel a peculiar pleasure in being thus the channel of conveying this honour to you.

You come from a great family, great in the annals of Calcutta, I may say great in the annals of the British Dominions in India, conspicuous for loyalty to the British Government and for acts of public beneficence.

But it is not from a consideration for your family alone the Viceroy has been pleased to confer this high honour upon you. You have proved yourself worthy of it by your own merits. Your great intelligence, ability, distinguished public spirit, high character, and the services which you have rendered to the State deserve a fitting recognition.

I have had the pleasure of receiving your assistance as a member of the Bengal Council, and can assure you that I highly appreciate the ability and information which you bring to bear upon its deliberations. Indeed, nothing can be more acceptable to me than advice from one like yourself. It is true we have had occasions to differ, and honest differences of opinion will always prevail between man and man, but at the same time I can honestly tell you that when we have been on the same side I have felt your support to be of the utmost value, and when you have chanced to be in opposition, yours has been an intelligent, loyal and courteous opposition,

I commend your example to your countrymen. If they will strive as you have done, they may be similarly honoured. May you live long and enjoy the honor."

Kristo Das who possessed a remarkable memory, reproduced it, and before its publication in the *Patriot*, it was shewn to Sir George for correction and improvement. Sir George was astonished at his speech being thus reproduced with such minuteness and congratulated Kristo Das on his marvellous performance.

THE STUDY OF POETRY IN OUR SCHOOLS AND COLLEGES, SIR GEORGE CAMPBELL AND KRISTO DAS.

It was during the administration of Sir George Campbell, that Mr. Atkinson, the then Director of Public Instruction in Bengal had a long quarrel with the Lieutenant Governor regarding High Education in Bengal. Sir George, though by far the ablest among our Lieutenant Governors, had his hobbies which he would some times ride to death, and various were the proposals made by him for the curtailment of the expenditure on High Education in Bengal as well as for lowering the status of the Calcutta Sanskrit College.

Once he took it into his head to prohibit the study of poetry in our schools and so he wrote to Mr. Atkinson a letter for the purpose. The Director knew well the temperament of Sir George, and thinking that any remonstrance on his part might do more harm than good, he privately requested Kristo Das to notice the fact in the columns of the *Hindoo Patriot*, as he knew well, that a paragraph on the subject therein, might induce the Lieutenant Governor to withdraw his proposal. Kristo Das at first hesitated to write on the subject, on the ground of its being a secret and confidential one, and that it might do harm to Mr. Atkinson himself. The matter being insisted on, the following paragraph appeared, which had the desired effect.

"Not content with waging a crusade against Sanskrit, Urdu, and Bengali, the Lieutenant Governor, we hear, contemplates to suppress the study of poetry in our schools! Oh! Ye Gods! witness this ruthless attack on the "faculty divine," and avenge it! What right has a profane ruler, who domineers over the official foolscap and dull prose to interdict the worship of the heavenly Muses, and can it be stopped even if he banishes poetry from the schools? Has the Lieutenant Governor the power to change the course of studies prescribed by the University?

His Honour, it is said, has no soul for the fine Arts. He hates poetry, painting and music. Perhaps this feeling of his accounts for his not patronizing the Fine Arts Exhibition at the Dalhousie Institute. We care not for his personal tastes and feelings, but it would be dangerous if he should allow them to influence his action as the ruler of the land. Poetry is to be banished from our schools! What next and next? Putting the claims of poetry on cold utilitarian ground we would address His Honour in the following lines of Pope—

> What can a boy learn sooner than a song ?
> What better teach the foreigner the tongue ?
> What's long and short, each accent to place,
> And speak in public with some sort of grace ?"
>
>   *A. Pope.*

KRISTO DAS PAL'S REJOINDER TO THE ATTACK ON THE HINDOO PATRIOT BY SIR GEORGE, THE LIEUTENANT GOVERNOR OF BENGAL.

Kristo Das as a journalist opposed almost every measure taken by Sir George Campbell during his administration of Bengal. Sir George was a man of radical ideas, and wanted to govern Bengal in a way opposed to its traditions. The *Hindoo Patriot* as the leading organ opposed every measure taken by the Lieutenant Governor regarding High Education, Mass Education; Parallel Line of Promotion, Subordinate Executive Service and other matters of local interest. Week after week, the columns of the *Hindoo Patriot* contained strong remarks on these and other cognate subjects, and Sir George was much hampered by the honest but bold criticisms of his measures made by Kristo Das Pal. The Bengal Government therefore considered him to cherish "ill will towards Government." In the Resolution of the Lieutenant Governor reviewing the Annual General Report of the Presidency Commissioner for 1872-1873, the Lieutenant Governor characterized the *Hindoo Patriot* as a pretentious paper cherishing "ill will towards Government." To this Kristo Das replied in a long letter from which we make the following extracts :—

To
H. LUTTMAN-JOHNSON ESQ.,
Private Secretary to His Honor the Lieutenant Governor of Bengal.

SIR,

IT is with much reluctance that I venture to address you this letter. But deeply aggrieved as I feel by certain remarks, which occur in the Resolution of the Hon'ble the Lieutenant Governor, reviewing the annual general Report of the Presidency Commissioner for 1872-73, dated the 22nd October, and published in the *Calcutta Gazette* for the 5th November last, I find, I have no alternative left me."

"The Native Press labors under peculiar disadvantages. It has not the same access to information which the English Press has; it necessarily relies upon native informants, who are themselves not always well-informed, and who cannot always express themselves in a way, which will not render them liable to misconstruction of motives; while it discusses principles of measures, so far as they may be applicable to the circumstances of the country, its usefulness chiefly lies in the delineation of the working of the laws enacted, and of the courts administering those laws, in the guaging of the pressure of taxation, in the exposure of abuses of power and caprices of individual officers, in the representation of the feelings of the people as the aggregate effect of the different agencies and influences in operation."

"I am somewhat surprized to observe that complaint is made against the Native Press because it now and then contains attacks against native officers. This statement, I respectfully submit, is the best evidence that the Native Press is doing its duty. It shews that it makes no distinction of race or religion in criticising the conduct of public officers. And the effect of such criticism, I need hardly remark, cannot but be healthy. It is the proud privilege of the Press to co-operate with the Government in correcting the vagaries of headstrong, ill-informed, idle, and self-willed officers, and if that power be taken away, it altogether ceases to be an instrument of good. In short what is set down as the fault of the Press constitutes, in my humble opinion, its strong point of usefulness."

"The remarks which I have ventured to make in regard to the Native Press generally, apply equally to the *Hindoo Patriot*. I have been the responsible editor of this paper for the last thirteen years, and whatever its imperfections, of which none can be more conscious than myself, this is the first time that it has been charged with shewing " ill will to Government." I have already said that in the absence of grounds, or data in support of the charge, I am not in a position to meet it; but I challenge any person to point out a single passage or expression in the mass of writings that have appeared in this journal, which can be interpreted into " ill will to Government," that is to say, to the British Government as an entity, to the authority of the gracious Sovereign, under whose beneficent sway it is our privilege and happiness to live."

With regard to the *Patriot* I would solicit His Honor to recall to mind one incident. In the beginning of August 1872, you invited me to meet His Honor, and in the interview which I had with him he was pleased to call my attention to certain remarks of two vernacular papers, in which it was insinuated that certain favors shewn by him to the Mahomedans had proceeded from a " fear of the knife." So far as I recollect the conversation at this hour, His Honor prefaced by saying, that he was aware of differences of opinion between the *Patriot* and the Bengal Government on many important questions, but, addressing me, His Honor continued, "I know you are a loyal man, and you do not certainly approve of these insinuations. The Government might take harsh measures against these papers, but it does not choose to do so. If you, as the leader of the Native Press, will co-operate with the Government and bring your influence to bear upon the vernacular press, I dare say the evil will correct itself." I at once expressed my indigation at the unjust insinuations made by the two vernacular papers in question, and offered my humble service to Government to counteract, as much as lay within my power, this evil tendency in the vernacular press. With regard to the *Patriot* I ventured to assure His Honor that he could always rely upon its loyal co-operation, though it might take exception to those measures of the Government, to which it could not conscientiously subscribe. His Honor was pleased to say that he had the fullest confidence in the loyalty of the *Patriot*, and that having that confidence he had thought it proper to speak to me on the subject. In the next number of the *Patriot* I gave an article reproducing the extracts marked by His Honor, condemning the spirit breathing through them, and warning the vernacular press generally against the practice of "using language," as I said, "which was not warranted by the exigencies of political controversy, nor calculated to do any good, but on the contrary positive harm." "Such insinuations," the article went on to say, " were most unjust to the head of the Local Government. We could believe that the writers we have quoted did not quite mean what their words would imply, but such thoughtless expressions were apt to be exaggerated, and cited by our enemies to our own detriment." I also took occasion to impress this truth upon the writers concerned by verbal communications. Since then, it, is gratifying to state, I have not noticed in any native paper such unjust and reckess insinuations."

"In conclusion, I solicit the favour of your submitting this letter to His Honour for such notice as he may think fit to take of it. I venture to entertain an earnest hope that on a perusal of the above statements and facts His Honor will be graciously pleased to exonerate the *Patriot* from the serious and, as I have attempted to shew, unfounded charge that has been brought against it. Should this not be the case, I solicit that a copy of the statements or data on which the charge is based may be furnished me, that I may be enabled to offer such explanations regarding them as may be in my power to submit to His Honor. I also solicit His Honor's permission to publish this letter together with your reply, if you will have the kindness to favour me with one.

I have the honor to be.
Sir,
Your obedient Servant.
Kristodas Pal,
Editor, Hindoo Patriot.

Calcutta,
Hidoo Patriot Press,
The 22nd December, 1873.

REPLY.

BELVEDERE, ALIPORE.
The 23*rd December* 1873.

MY DEAR BABU,

The Lieutenant Governor has read with interest your remarks on the loyalty to Government displayed by your paper the *Hindoo Patriot*. He is much pleased to hear that you do not bear to Government the ill will which the Commissioner of the Presidency Division attributed to your paper.

I remain,
MY DEAR BABU,
Yours faithfully,
H. L. JOHNSON,
Private Secretary.

Babu Kristo Das Pal,
Hindoo Patriot Office
Calcutta.

SIR GEORGE CAMPBELL'S ADMINISTRATION AND KRISTO DAS PAL.

Kristo Das reviewed the administration of Sir George in a series of very able articles which were published in 1874 in a pamphlet form. The opening article began thus.

"THE usual Five Acts (or Five Years) Drama of an Indian Governor's administration has been cut short, in the case of Sir George Campbell, at the author's pleasure, to Three Acts (or Three years), and the last Act is about to close. The highest praise, which we can accord to the author, who is himself the hero as well as the chief actor, is that he has not allowed the interest of the play to flag for a single moment. The most brilliant efforts of Kean or Kemble, Mrs. Siddons or Macready were not more attractive or more exciting than the matter-of-fact performances of the retiring Lieutenant-Governor of Bengal. Every word he has uttered, every line he has written, every act he has performed, shew that he has done so with an eye to dramatic effect, and his success in producing a temporary flutter has been immense. What the permanent effects of his administrative ventures will be it is impossible to foresee—whether these ventures will be allowed to run their legitimate course it is also difficult to anticipate. But one thing is clear—in performing his part he has displayed a mental power, energy, and activity, which are really marvellous. Bengal had never before had a Governor, whose mind was so richly stored with varied knowledge, though necessarily superficial, who combined such a vigorous mind for grasping principles with such an enormous capacity for working out details, and who made his power so universally felt through the length and breadth of his dominions, by the rich and the poor, the educated and the uneducated, the high civilian and the lowly native myrmidon alike. When he ascended the throne of Belvedere we expected great things from him: for the first few months we waited with anxious expectancy. Constituted as his mind was, many days did not, however, pass away when we had evidence of its erratic course; still we would not believe our eyes or ears, still we thought that we were mistaken, that our informants were mistaken, that our observant countrymen were mistaken. We argued with those, who sought to correct us, that he could have but one object in view, viz., the good of the people; that if he was ambitious, ambition was the noblest infirmity of man's mind; that if he seemed to be obstinate, decision of character was an essential qualification in a ruler of men; that if he had a prejudice against Bengal ideas and Bengal men, it would wear off with time; that if he was restless, he would himself become tired and seek rest, and so on."

The second article was on the "Changes in the Administration," the third, on "Land Policy," the fourth, on "Criminal Justice, Police, and Prison," the fifth on "Civil Justice, Educated Natives and Lawyers," the sixth on "Education," the seventh on "Principles of Government, the Press and the People," the eighth on "Famine," and the ninth and last was to bid "Adieu to Sir George."

As we have not space for copious extracts from these articles we extract the following from the last.

ADIEU !

"We now bid ADIEU to Sir George Campbell. It is a word always painful to utter, and yet it must be uttered some time or other. What, however, adds to the pang of regret which we feel, is the circumstances under which he leaves this country. It is always a pleasing spectacle to see a ruler of many millions lay down his charge amid the blessings of those whom he came to govern. But alas! how differently blessed the man who wielded the sceptre of Bengal for the last three years. If he came to make a name, he leaves a name which will be a warning to many coming after him. Like an Ishmaelite his hand was against every body, and every bodie's hand against him. There is scarcely a class of this vast community, with which he has not managed to be unpopular. He has been unpopular with his own service, which at one time, according to his own statement in the Administration Report, threatened to rise in rebellion against him. He has been unpopular with the uncovenanted service, because he has given away its prizes to covenanted assistants, degraded its position, lowered emoluments, and freezed its independence. He has been unpopular with the educational service, the members of which he has repeatedly insulted by ill-merited snubs and reproofs. He has been unpopular with the judicial service, the members of which from the highest to the lowest he has missed no pretext to attack and lower in the estimation of the public by an arrogant assertion of executive authority. He has been unpopular with the departmental heads, whom he has sought to reduce to the position of correspondence clerks. He has been unpopular with the University authorities by waging a crusade against their legitimate authority and even questioning their intelligence. He has been unpopular with the medical profession by casting aspersions upon their Income-tax returns and subverting the reforms in prisons, which the representatives of that faculty had effected after years of thought, labour, and struggle. He has been unpopular with the representatives of the legal profession, whom he has literally abused in season and out of season. He has been unpopular with the independent Europeans, for whose opinions and sentiments he has shewn the utmost contempt. He has been unpopular with the zemindars, whom he has denounced from his high place as "wolves." He has been unpopular with the ryots, whom he has saddled with an oppressive cess, and upon whom he sought to impose many more taxes, and would have succeeded but for the humane interference of His Excellency the Viceroy, for whose health and life he shewed the most cruel indifference by his utter inaction to remove the causes of the fell epidemic fever, which has for years been decimating the fairest villages in Bengal, though repeatedly urged to do so, and against whose personal liberty he set a determined face by allowing the police and the magistrates to indulge in their freaks and caprices, and by destroying those safeguards against abuse of power which the old law provided. And, lastly, he has been unpopular with the educated classes of the native community, by putting them down with a high hand, by fighting against their legitimate aspirations, by aspersing their character, and by prejudicing them in the estimation of the good and true." *. *

"Who can doubt such amiable assurances? He has set class against class, and that has been done out of pure sympathy with the people. He has minuted against the appointment of educated natives to the covenanted civil service, and that has been done out of pure sympathy with the people. He has pursued with an unappeasable wrath a hapless black youth, who had the audacity to enter the sacred preserves of his service, for faults which the Civilians themselves admit are more the faults of the system than of the individual, while he has condoned several white youths charged with far graver faults, and that has been done out of pure sympathy with the people. He has not scrupled to subsidize Christian Missionaries to destroy traces of Hinduism among the aboriginal tribes, and to outrage the religious feelings of the Hindus by threatening their Car festival, and that has been done out of pure sympathy with the people. He turned a deaf ear to an appeal of the nation to exercise the Queen's prerogative of mercy in the case of a poor native prisoner, who under an impulse, with which all right-minded men sympathized, did an act which the law certainly condemned, but in favour of which the highest Court in the land admitted there were many extenuating circumstances, and that was done out of pure sympathy with the people. He has reviled the organs of native opinion and proposed to take away from it the means of proper ventilation, which the beneficent policy of Lord Canning conferred upon it, and that has been done out of pure sympathy with the people. He snatched away from our youths the opportunity of studying in the school the sacred tongue of their forefathers, and banished the Bengali language from provinces which were content to receive it as their own, and which could hope to grow into a compact nationality only by speaking and writing a common tongue, and that has been done out of pure sympathy with the people."

The Mahesh Ruth Festival and Babu Kristo Das Pal.

Babu Kristo Das rendered important services to the Hindu Community of Bengal, on three different occasions. He first protected the proprietors of the Mohesh Car from the "crusade," the officials waged against its dragging; secondly he helped the Hindoos of Pandua to celebrate their Durga Puja Festival unmolested; and thirdly he lent his assistance in the matter of keeping intact the number of Doorga Pooja Holidays.

During the administrations of Sir George Campbell and Sir Richard Temple, various attempts had been made to suppress the dragging of the Car on the ground of public safety. It was in 1874 that the dragging of the Car was actually disallowed by the local authorities, on the first day of the Festival. On the Ulta Ruth (return journey) day, fresh objections were raised on the ground of its not being well repaired. Although the priests got the Car fully repaired as testified to by M. Bradford Leslie, the local authorities remained inexorable and the ceremony was put a stop to. In this dilemma Babu Nemy Churn Bose the representative of the Founder of the Car came to Babu Kristo Das for help. What Kristo Das did, we shall relate in his own words :—

"Babu Nemye Churn Bose was helpless, for if that day was allowed to slip away in the same manner as was the first day of the festival, there would be no ceremony for the year. As both the Commissioner and the Lieutenant Governor were on tour (on Famine duty) he did not know what to do. He returned (from Scrampore) to Calcutta and was advised to petition His Excellency the Governor General; it was half past two when Babu Nemy Churn had returned to Calcutta, and in two hours time a petition was drafted, engrossed, and presented to his excellency."

Kristo Das personally saw Lord Northbrook and spoke to him on the subject.

Lord Northbrook first hesitated to pass an order in the matter, on the ground of its being a local question which should be decided by the Lieutenant Governor, but on further representation, a telegram was sent to the local authorities and the Car was allowed to be drawn.

DURGA PUJA AT PANDUA AND BABU KRISTO DAS PAL.

Pandua is situated in the District of Hoogly on the E. I. Railway. What Jerusalem is to Christianity, what Mecca is to Islamism, and what Benares is to the Hindus, so Pandua is to the Mahomedans of Bengal. In this city of Mahomedanism, the Hindus were not allowed, so far back ago as 1823, to perform worship according to their time honoured custom by carrying idols through the streets for immersion, which is a necessary part of the ceremonies observed. To remove this disability, repeated attempts had been made in times gone by, in vain. The late Babu Muty Lal Seal (the Prince of Native Merchants) engaged Mr. Longueville Clarke to plead the cause of Pandua 'Hindus but without success. The Pandua Mahomedans having had great influence with the big civilians, every attempt made in this direction proved abortive.

It fell to the lot of Babu Kristo Das, however, to get this disability removed at last. He took up the cause of the aggrieved and wrote in 1876, a petition for them to Sir Richard Temple, then Lieutenant Governor of Bengal, and in a series of articles in the *Hindoo Patriot*, dwelt upon their grievances. Sir Richard through the influence of Babu Kristo Das removed this perpetual interdiction.

THE BARODA QUESTION AND THE
HON'BLE KRISTO DAS PAL.

On the death of Khandi Rao in 1870, his brother Mulhar Rao was taken from the prison and placed on the throne. Kristo Das thus wrote about him in 1875:—" No one can deny that grave abuses had crept into the administration of that state since Mulhar Rao under British protection marched from the prison-house to the throne. Without experience, without any of the virtues, which distinguished his brother, with a most fickle character, and a tool in the hands of corrupt intriguers he had not one qualification for the throne, which he was called upon to fill, and we were not therefore surprised that abuse and oppression became the order of the day under his rule. Petitions against his rule were presented to the Viceroy and the cry became so loud that His Excellency could not help making an enquiry into the charges against the Gwekwar. Commission of enquiry was appointed, which after due investigation reported against His Highness; the Viceroy would not however hastily take an extreme step; he granted him grace for one year if the Gwekwar would make amends during the period he would allow him to rule."

Mulhar Rao was, in 1874, accused of having instigated an attempt to poison Colonel R. Phayre C. B., the British Resident at Baroda. He was tried by a High Commission composed of the Hon'ble

Sir Richard Couch, His Highness the Maharaja of Gwalior. His Highness the Maharajah of Joypur, Colonel Sir Richard John Meade, Rajah Sir Dinkur Rao, and Philip Sandys Melville. Esq.

That Kristo Das supported every step of Lord Northbrook will be apparent from the following extract :—

"We are not surprized that the greatest diversity of opinions prevails on the subject of the proceedings of Government regarding Boroda. At the same time we think the Government should not be too sensitive nor its critics too nice. The main object of the Government ought to command the approval of all right thinking men. It is the protection of the interests of the people of Baroda, which has formed the primary object of our Government from the beginning of this enquiry, we mean the first as well as the present. As for the deposition of the Gwekwar we do not believe that it is a foregone conclusion. Lord Northbrook has disarmed the annexationists by declaring that whatever may be the result of the present trial, the State shall be restored to a Native Administration. The old days of annexation are not to be revived—they have passed away we hope for ever. If the Gwekwar be found guilty of the atrocious charge laid against him, let him suffer but nothing that he had done will justify the absorption of his State, and Lord Northbrook has in a most straight forward and emphatic manner declared that he contemplates no such *denouement.*"

The Lokenathpore Case.

The history of this case, so far as it relates to the part played therein, by Babu Kristo Das Pal, will simply serve to shew that when opportunity presented itself, he was always ready to help the poor, and to protect them from the oppression to which they are at times subjected in this country. His sympathy was of a universal kind. Although by the peculiar circumstances of his life, he had to associate mainly with the aristocracy of the land, he never imbibed that spirit of superciliousness towards the poor which such association generally produces in a mind not sufficiently strong in moral and intellectual qualities. Kristo Das was a friend alike to the rich and the poor. The facts which we are going to relate here will clearly establish the truth, that though he was by birth and education, habit and association, a citizen of Calcutta, he never lacked the sympathy for those helpless beings who resided beyond the pale of the Maharatta Ditch.

It was in the summer months of 1876, that the dead body of a man named Ramguty Biswas was found floating in a tank close to an Indigo Factory then known as the Lokenathpore Concern. It is situated a few miles off from the Joyrampore Railway Station on the Eastern Bengal State Railway in the District of Nuddea. It was believed at the time by the relatives of the deceased and the general local public, that he was murdered at the Factory, while the officials believed that the deceased committed "malicious suicide." An extra-judicial enquiry was made at the time into this matter, and after an elaborate and careful but secret investigation, it was decided by the officials that he was not murdered by any body, but that he put an end to his own life to serve his own wicked purpose. The survivors and relatives of the deceased were not satisfied with this official version, and they therefore wanted an open enquiry into the matter. The brother of the deceased first telegraphed to Sir Ashley Eden, the then Lieutenant-Governor of Bengal, who was residing in his summer retreat at Darjeeling, to order a fresh enquiry into the matter; but as is usual in this country, even this last expedient did not produce its desired effect, as Sir Ashley Eden had partially accepted the official theory of "malicious suicide."

Failing thus to obtain redress from the official quarter, the brother of the deceased who was an ignorant and illiterate villager, was then advised by his educated neighbours to see Babu Kristo Das Pal personally, at Calcutta, with a view to request him to notice the facts of the case in the columns of the *Hindoo Patriot*. The poor man had to travel a distance of nearly eighty miles to come from Joyrampore his native village to Calcutta, and to suffer great privations in order to have an interview with the Hon'ble Kristo Das Pal. Notwithstanding the high position which Kristo Das occupied in the Calcutta Society, he was possessed of such a genial nature and magnanimity of heart that he was accessible even to a common villager at any hour of the day. The brother of the deceased got easy access to him and represented his grievances. The following paragraph accordingly appeared in the *Hinddo Patriot* in July 1877 dealing with the facts of the case and calling public attention to it :—

"A case of diabolical murder has been brought to our notice, and we commend it to the earnest attention of the Magistrate of Nuddea and the sub-divisional officer of Choadanga, in whose jurisdiction it has occured. On the 9th instant at about 4 P.M., one Ramguty Biswas accompanied by another person named Troilokhonath Biswas started for the Factory at Lokenathpore in the Choadanga sub-division. At about 1 A.M. Troylokho returned and reported that Ramguty was detained at the factory for the satisfaction of the debt due to it. At 11 A.M. of the following day report was received at the Police station of Joyrampore, that a portion of Ramguty's garments together with his riding whip saddle and bridle was found under a tree near the Doogdoogy tullah or tank and that his horse was found tethered at a spot hard by but no trace found of the owner. In the subsequent police enquiry which followed the body was hauled up from the tank above named. It was sent to a hospital by the Police Inspector for examination, and the doctor reported that death was caused by the deceased being caught by the throat and struck on the face. We are informed that an enquiry was held at the factory by the Magistrate himself, and a similar enquiry was held at Sreekole, the native village of the deceased, by the

Inspector of the Damoorhooda police station, to ascertain by personal examination of the party who accompanied Ramguty, the fact of the deceased journey in his company, and the return of the deponent without the deceased. Six other persons of the village were also examined. No clue has been found of the murderer. This is scandalous. It would reflect no credit upon the Police and the Magistrates, if the author of such an atrocity should go undetected and unpunished."

The *Hindoo Patriot* was then in the hey-day of its glory, and as such its writings were carefully perused by the officials of the land. No sooner had the paragraph appeared than it attracted the attention of those who were immediately concerned in it. An official contradiction was immediately sent by a civilian under the *nom-de plume* of "Veritas."

The contradiction runs thus :—

"Sir,—The remarks contained in your issue of the 2nd July regarding the recent occurrence near Lokenathpore Factory have caused considerable surprise to those acquainted with the facts. "Scandalous" is a strong word to apply to official misconduct, however, gross and well proved. What shall be said then to the application of such an epithet, when, in point of fact, the local officers have strained every nerve to solve the mystery, and when, in spite of the greatest difficulties, the truth has at last come to light, and every circumstance attending the decease of the Ramguty Biswas is accurately known. In the interests of common justice I would ask you to refrain from further comment of the kind you have indulged in, till you are put in possession of the facts by the publication of the proceedings of the local officers ; and in the meantime, it is no breach of official etiquette to assure you that the information on which you based your strictures is the reverse of the fact in every material particular. I enclose my card."

Your Obedient Servant,
"Veritas."

The contradiction of the editorial statement by "Veritas" left Kristo Das no choice whatever to write anything more on the subject without being fully assured of the real facts of the case. So Kristo Das remained silent and wrote us a private letter to be on the look out for a fresh clue to this mysterious matter.

Months had elapsed before it was possible to know the secrets of the case. After an interval of 4 or 5 months we got a clue to the official secrets, and agreeably with the request of Babu Kristo Das Pal, we communicated the following news published in the columns of the *Hindoo Patriot* of the 17th September 1877 :—

When the case was first noticed by you, "Veritas," who seemed to be an official, intimately acquainted with the facts of it, stopped your mouth by promising an early publication of the official report thereon. Although nearly more than two months have elapsed, since his letter dated Calcutta 6th July, 1877, appeared in the *Hindoo Patriot* of the 9th instant, we have not been favoured with the promised report and knew nothing of the facts of the case, except the official order to prosecute

Troyloko Nath Biswas and Ramguty Kabar, for giving false evidence in the matter. Mr. Taylor of Maherpore has been ordered to proceed to Choondanga and to sit in judgment over the two delinquents, and sundry rumours are afloat anent this prosecution, and I may mention that the people of this district have been taken aback that while not a line has been published by Government solving the mystery of the death, the two witnesses in question are being prosecuted."

The case was thus for the second time noticed in the *Hindoo Patriot* and the trial which ensued, as a corollary to the first one, protracted its course for more than a year. It was Babu Kristo Das who took a personal interest in the case, and helped the friends of the defendants with advice and money as will be apparent from the following letter :—

18 British Indian Street,
Calcutta, the 28th January 1878.

My dear Sir,

Babu Kristo Das has received your letter of the 28th instant and sends herewith the second half of the five rupee note as his humble contribution to the Lokenathpore case defence fund. &c. &c. &c.

Yours truly,
Gopal Chunder Dutt.

To Babu Ram Gopal Sanyal.

We do not wish to enter into the details of the case for fear of trespassing upon the patience of our readers. Suffice it to say that it was Babu Kristo Das who suggested to us that Mr. Mon Mohun Ghose of the Calcutta Bar should be entreated to take up the case as an *amicus curae*.

Mr. Ghose and Babu Akhya Kumar Mukerjee the

well-known pleader of the Krishnaghur Bar got the poor defendants in the perjury case released from two months rigorous imprisonment; and it was Babu Kristo Das who persuaded the members of the British Indian Association to raise a fund of Rs. 500 amongst themselves, in order to defray the cost of bringing up the case before the High Court of Calcutta. The following gentlemen subscribed to the fund :—

	Rs.	As.	P.
Babu Joykissen Mukerjee Zemindar Otterparah	50	0	0
Sir Maharaja Jotendro Mohun Tagore K.C.S.I.	50	0	0
The late Kumar Kanti Chunder Sing Bahadur Paikpara	50	0	0
The late Hon'ble Babu Digambur Mitter C.I.E.	50	0	0
Maharajah Kali Kissen Bahadoor	100	0	0
The Hon'ble Durga Churn Law, C.I.E....	50	0	0

Thus it was that Babu Kristo Das vindicated the good name of the British Indian Association by making them subscribe to a fund which was devoted to the sacred purpose of bringing out two innocent men from Jail. These helpless men would have been incarcerated, had not Kristo Das Pal used his influence, agreeably with the request of Mr. Ghose, to raise money for their help. The British Indian Association is often reproached as a body having no sympathy with the poor, the reproach is most unjust.

Birth-day Honours.

In 1877 Kristo Das was honoured with the title of "Rai Bahadur" in recognition of his meritorious public services. He felt grateful to the Government no doubt for the honour done to him, but as these titular distinctions were not much thought of by the public, Kristo Das, as a matter of course, did not feel proud of it. He thus wrote on the subject:—

"We are not a little surprised to find our own name among the Rai Bahadurs. If we may be allowed to be light-hearted on such a solemn subject, may we ask what dire offence did we commit, for which this punishment was reserved for us. We have no ambition for titular distinctions; we are a humble worker in the service of the nation, and would be quite content, if we could but obtain the approbation of our own conscience and that of our fellow-countrymen and fellow-creatures, aye, also of the powers that be, in the discharge of our function as a faithful interpreter between the rulers and the ruled and *vice versa*. For our part we are proud of the name of *Hindoo Patriot*, which we have the honor to bear, and we hope we will not be accused of a braggart spirit, if we say that if we can act up to our name, as we endeavour to do, the highest honor which can fall to our lot will be ours. We are certainly grateful to the Government for this token of appreciation and approbation of our humble services, but if we had had a voice in the matter, we would have craved the permission of our kind and generous rulers to leave us alone and unadorned, following the footsteps of those honored and illustrious Englishmen, by whose side we are but pigmies, who have preferred to remain without a handle to their names. We hope we will not be misunderstood. As a loyal subject, we repeat, we feel deeply grateful to Her Majesty's Government for this token of Her gracious approbation, but we hope we will be pardoned for giving expression to our personal feelings."

The Meherpur Case.

Following in the wake of the Lokenathpore case, Kristo Das brought the above case to the light of publicity. As a journalist he sought information on every subject from every quarter, and did not disdain to obtain it even from men of humble pretensions. When we informed him privately as a correspondent of the *Hindoo Patriot*, that a failure of justice had taken place, he advised us confidentially to take copies of the records of the case in order to publish them in the columns of the *Patriot*. On our asking him to help us with money to obtain authenticated copies of the records, he advised us to spend a residue of the Lokenathpore case fund which was then at our disposal, for the above purpose. We then obtained copies of the records which were published in the *Hindoo Patriot* :—

"Another mysterious murder is reported from the district of Nuddea. It was committed in the sub-division of Meherpore. The facts of the case are contained in the following depositions before and the judgment of Mr. Taylor, the Joint-Magistrate, whom the reader might recognize as the Solon, who convicted the two unfortunate witnesses in the Lokenathpore case."

In this case the prisoners have been charged by the police with the murder of one Munsaff Sheik.

The circumstances of the case are as follows :— "It appears that the deceased was fined by Mr. White, a planter, and asked the defendants to intercede for him, the second defendant being the servant and the first defendant being supposed to possess some influence with him. The deceased followed the planter to a distant factory and reached the village in the afternoon or about noon and went to seek the first defendant, whose house is close to the factory. He returned after a fruitless search of his relative Golam Sheik, and they went again but again fruitlessly to see Jadu in the evening. Next morning Golam went to his work and the deceased expressed his intention of visiting Jadu. Shortly after this Golam states that he heard Jadu calling his own name "Golam come here Munsaff is drowned," and adds that on running up he found Munsaff lying with his head under water, but the rest of his body on the ooze of the bank. When taken up he was quite dead. The medical evidence ascribes his death to rupture of the spleen. The only evidence beyond what I have stated is that of Matam Molla, who states that he saw the defendant Jadu and three others throw the body into the Khal, he himself being on the opposite side of the water. When the police sent up the case, the witness Mamlat Sheik had given a circumstantial account of the murder of the deceased by the two defendants and some other under the direction of Mr. White. This deposition he afterwards retracted and denied all knowledge of the affair. The evidence then as it stands is exceedingly week whether owing to the influence of the Zemindar and his servants or not, I cannot say. But it is so weak that I do not feel justified in committing the prisoners to take their trial upon it, especially upon so grave a charge."

The defendants are discharged under section 195 of C. P. C.

(Sd.) F. B. TAYLOR,
Offg. Joint-Magistrate.

24-11-1877.

Empress vrs., Mamlat Sheik.

The petitioner is a youth and it is clear that on whichever side his falsehood lies, he was influenced by some one or other to make that statement. As it is impossible to prove the truth or falsehood of either of his statements he may be released from bail.

(Sd.) F. B. TAYLOR.

24-11-1877.

"So this murder remains wholly unaccounted for. We leave it to the reader to say whether the enquiry made was sufficient. We hear that Mr. Stevens, the District Magistrate, since the Lokenathporo case agitation, is satisfied that the enquiry has not been sufficient and that he is disposed to hold a second enquiry. We therefore withhold further comments."

On the publication of these records, the attention of the Government was drawn to it, and the local officials were at last obliged to make a fresh enquiry into the matter. Mr. White was again brought to trial, and committed to the Calcutta High Court Sessions. In due time Justice Pontifex presided over the sessions, and the defendant was, after a regular trial, discharged and acquitted for want of sufficient evidence.

Dr. Mahendralal Sircar's Science Association.

Kristo Das was ever ready to accord his support to those projects for national improvement which had been taken in hand by such public spirited men as Dr. Mahendra Lal Sircar. Narrowness of views or prejudice he had none; he saw things in their true light and as a man of "leading and light" he used to help those institutions of the country not only by dwelling upon their utility in his journal, but also by giving direct assistance to the originators of these movements.

Dr. Mahendra Lal Sircar conceived the idea of establishing the Association. The idea was a grand one; he stood in need of public support to carry out that idea. Kristo Das helped him materially in this noble project. Having great influence over the zemindars of Bengal, he induced many of them to contribute to the fund required by Dr. Sircar for the establishment of his Association.

Dr. Mahendra Lal Sircar M. D., thus alluded to the service rendered to the establishment of the Science Association in his memorable speech delivered at its inaugural meeting held on 29th July 1876 :—

"To you. Babu Kristo Das (the Hon'ble Kristo Das), many thanks for the friendly care with which you have nursed the scheme, and I felt it my duty here to declare publicly, that without your friendly and patriotic nursing the scheme would have died the death of a premature birth; at least, would never have attained shape and dimensions enough to attract public sympathy and support. And I must also take this opportunity to return my sincere thanks to the press of India for their unanimous and powerful advocacy of the project."

The Chittagong Case.

The secret Resolution of Sir Richard Temple on this case censuring and removing Mr. Kirkwood from Chittagong for grave direlection of duty was published by Kristo Das in the issue of the *Hindoo Patriot* of 28th August 1876. Its publication produced an alarming sensation in the country, and enhanced the reputation of his paper. The *Statesman* insinuated that Kristo Das got it surreptitiously to which he replied as follows:—

"Speculation is rife as to how we got the now celebrated Resolution of the Lieutenant-Governor anent Mr. Kirkwood, and our contemporary of the *Statesman* goes to the length of charging us with "surreptitiously" obtaining it. That is not the right word, good brother. We are not bound to say how we got the Resolution, but we may state for the information of those, whom it may concern, that it came to our hands quite unexpectedly. It was brought to us by a gentleman in this city, who gave us full authority to publish it. More we need not say. We would not have been true to our name and profession, if we had not given it to the public."

The Vernacular Press Act.

On Thursday forenoon the 14th March 1878, the Vernacular Press Act was enacted into law. Long before the enactment of this law, Kristo Das was several times requested by Sir George Campbell and other high officials of the land, to exercise his influence over some of his native contemporaries in moderating their tone. This he did on occasions more than one. While he admonished his brother contemporaries for their occasional intemperate use of language towards Government, he never hesitated to vindicate the character of the native Press in general from the aspersions of the officials. On the enactment of this law he wrote a leading article on the subject from which we make the following extract :—

"'The best proof of the manner in which England has fulfilled her solemn trust and noble mission is afforded in the contrast which one may run and read in the condition of the people under British rule and the administration of the Native Princes. Indeed, not a little of the improvement now observable in the native states is due to the salutary influence of the superior system of British administration in such close proximity."

Dwelling thus on the blessings of the British administration, he again said :—

"After enjoying this boon for about forty-three years a portion of the people of this country are deprived of it. Could a greater misfortune befall the country than this ? A law was passed at one sitting on Thursday last by His Excellency the Viceroy in Council for the restriction of the Vernacular Press. . . . And when it is remembered that the Government is now presided over by a statesman, who is himself a votary of literature, and an advocate of free speech and writing, and that he takes the responsibility of the measure, the reader may rest assured that His Excellency would not have moved in the matter, without good and valid reasons. It cannot be denied that the fate; which has overtaken the Vernacular Press, is greatly due to the follies and indiscretions of many of its unworthy members. These had sufficient warning, which they heeded not. They went on in their devil-me-care spirit, regardless of consequences."

Saying thus much by way of disparagement to the ill-disposed portion of the native Press, he criticized the policy of the Government thus :—

"So far we believe there can be no reasonable difference of opinion. But the question is whether the safety of the empire requires the form of law, which has been just passed. Are the worst vernacular papers more violent than the rabid Irish papers, and have these been suppressed ? Are the Indians more excitable than the Irish, and yet are the Irish interfered with ? Dr. Kenealy's *Englishman*, Reynolds' *Miscellany*, *Vanity Fair* and the *World* contain worse things, which are read by more excitable populations, but the English Government does not think it necessary to put them down."

He thus concluded his first article on the subject :—

"Upon the whole we are convinced, and we say this with all humility, that the Government was ill-advised in pushing the Bill through with such unseemly haste. It is of course useless now to discuss its merits or the mode of its enactment. We, however, do hope that now that the bill has become law it will be worked with consideration and moderation. The Government has the giant's strength, but we should be much mistaken if it should use it as a giant."

In April 1878 a large public meeting was held in the Town Hall of Calcutta to protest against this law. Kristo Das who sympathized with the object of the meeting could not attend it. He however wrote a very long article in support of it from which we extract the following :—

"Last Wednesday's meeting, supplemented as we hope it will be, by similar meetings in other parts of of the country, cannot we feel convinced fail to move the generous sympathies of the English nation. Freedom of speech is the key-stone of the British constitution, and the birth-right of the British subject wherever placed, and will not true-born Britons defend it when it is assailed in India ? We have ample confidence that they will."

On the repeal of the Vernacular Press Act in 1881, he wrote an article with great humour and ability, from which we extract the following :—

"It has devolved upon Lord Ripon to give burial to some of the monstrous births that took place at the time of his predecessor. He has already given burial to the Afghan policy of Lord Lytton and is about to perform the melancholy task in regard to the Vernacular Press Act. The last-mentioned monster, it may be said, has died of sheer inanition. No one has nursed it, no one has dandled it. It came into the world under unnatural circumstances. It was conceived and brought forth almost on a single day. Those who assisted in the accouchment were taken quite unawares. The childlabour was easy enough, but those who watched the presentation were not without misgivings and mistrust. Poor Sir Alexander Arbuthnot was made to deliver it, but the child had two fathers in Sir John Strachey and Lord Lytton. As soon as the child was born, it was wrapped up in flannel, but it has never had regular sucking. As long as Lord Lytton was in the country, he gave it a suck now and then, but it has since simply withered away. Lord Ripon would not condescend to look upon the child, a hideous birth of a heated imagination. Want of nourishment has killed the child, and his Lordship has ordered a decent burial for it."

The Text-Book Committee.

Lord Lytton issued an order dated the 23rd April 1877, for the appointment of a Committee consisting of the Hon'ble E. S. Bayley as President, Mr. Tawney, Principal, Presidency College, Bengal, Mr. Thompson, Principal, Presidency College, Madras, Mr. Orenham, Principal, Deccan College, Poona, Bombay, Mr. Griffith, Principal, Benares College, N. W. P., Dr. Leitner, Principal, Lahore College, Punjab, as members and Mr. Loper Lethbridge, as Secretary. It was appointed to consider in detail the reports, suggestions, &c., made by the Provincial Committees appointed four years ago, and also to report on the production of vernacular text-books on law, jurisprudence, &c. To this Committee, Kristo Das was nominated by the Governor-General himself. In the latter end of May 1877, he went to Simla where the Committee assembled, and recorded an elaborate note for the consideration of the Committee dated 13th June 1877.

The Durga Pujah Holidays.

In the year 1861 the Bengal Chamber of Commerce made an attempt to curtail these holidays and made a representation to Government. A Committee was accordingly formed consisting of Mr. Harvey, Sub-Treasurer, Mr. W. S. Fitz-William, a member of the Chamber and the late Hon'ble Prosunno Kumar Tagore. This Committee recommended the grant of 32 days including a general holiday of

10 days during Durga Pujah. The Government of of India, in supercession of all previous orders, allowed 27 general holidays and 12 days for the Durga Puja. Some slight alterations were afterwards made in these holidays in 1862 and 1867.

In 1874 the Bengal Chamber again asked the Bengal Government to reduce the Doorga Puja holidays from 12 to 7 days, and in 1878 a further reduction was asked for, from 12 to 4 days. To settle this question a Committee was appointed by the Government composed of the Hon'ble H. L. Dampier, President, C. J. Brookes, Esq., W. D. Bruce, Esq., C.E., S. Cochrane, Esq., Babu Durga Churn Law, J. D. Maclean, Esq., the Hon'ble C. C. Morgan, Hon'ble Rai Kristo Das Pal Bahadur, C.I.E., G. Yule, Esq., F. W. Badcock, Esq., as Secretary. Babus Kristo Das and Durga Churn conjointly wrote a dissentient minute protesting against the proposal of the Chamber. It was through the exertion of Kristo Das that these holidays were allowed to be kept intact.

The Immigration Bill.

We have to allude to the opposition offered by Kristo Das to the enactment of the Act of 1881. The whole bill was conceived and concocted in the interest of the Planters and contained provisions prejudicial to those of the coolies. He characterized this law as the slave law of India and protested against the obnoxious clauses in a series of able articles. On the 14th December 1881 Kristo Das as Secretary to the British Indian Association submitted to the Viceroy a memorial on the subject regarding which the *Pioneer* made the following remarks :—

"The elaborate memorial against the Assam Labour Bill, presented to the Viceroy in Council at the last moment, goes minutely into details which no one but a specialist can appreciate. But at all events, it shows that the bill is open to a good deal of criticism, and from the point of view of the Bill—from the point of view, that is to say, of legislation aimed at putting stringent regulations on the employers of labour in Assam—a great deal of the criticism now put forward sounds intelligent. Assuming that the employers want to ill-treat a labourer and that the labourer is too stupid to take care of himself, it is evidently possible to conceive cases in which the Assam coolie would find the protection of the proposed law very insufficient."

Painful as it may be to us, we should be wanting in our duty if we failed to allude here to one unpleasant incident in connexion with it. In the course of a debate on this subject in the Viceregal Council, Sir Rivers Thompson characterised the attitude of the *Patriot* as "dishonest" and "dishonourable". We can only express the regret, and we are quite sure Sir Rivers Thompson himself will share the feeling with us that such language should have been used even in the excitement of debate. Kristo Das was not a man to be ruffled by these harsh words;

he kept his temper cool and wrote in the *Hindoo Patriot* as follows :—

"The dead cannot speak but the living ought. And because we have ventured to speak out, we have been called "dishonest" and "dishonourable", and charged with throwing "rhetorical mud." For the sake of the dumb and helpless labouring poor we are willing to take any amount of *galee*, decent or indecent."

The Contempt Case and the trial of Babu Surendranath Banerjea.

In 1883 Babu Surendranath Banerjea, Editor of the *Bengalee* was hauled up before the High Court of Calcutta for having made some reflections on Mr. Justice Norris in connexion with a case in which the Saligram idol of a Hindu suitor had been ordered into Court. The agitation that followed had a religious aspect in it. Kristo Das was requested by the officials of the land to allay public feeling so far as the religious aspect of the question was concerned, and wrote as follows :—

"The second point is the religious cry. We admit that the present agitation has acquired such a large volume, because there is religious feeling at the bottom. The agitation as we said last week has run like wild fire, from town to town, district to district, and province to province. And why, because the people of India are very sensitive in religious matters. Those who have taken part in the agitation have now come to know the real facts of the case. They cannot deny that it was not Mr. Justice Norris, who had taken the initiative in the matter. He had no personal interest in it, he had been moved by the parties interested, and he gave the orders after consulting too respectable Brahmins. So far Mr. Justice Norris did his duty. As far as he was individually concerned perhaps he would have done well, if he had, as we remarked in a previous issue, consulted his colleague, Mr. Justice Mitter, and, furthermore, if he had enquired what had been the practice of the Court in cases of this kind. But it might be urged that he was not bound to do all this. We are not bound to do many things, but as the world goes we take care to do what we are not bound to do as much for our own good as for the good of society Mr. Norris was not bound to consult his Brahmin interpreter, and yet he did consult him. But let that pass. At the same time we beg to assure our countrymen that our religion is not in danger. The Government has had nothing to do with the case. The policy of Government in matters of religion is open and aboveboard—it is one of strict neutrality. Our countrymen feel deeply grateful to Lord Ripon for his many beneficent measures, but they will do his Lordship a grievous injustice, if they for a moment think that his Government will do aught, which will outrage the religious feelings of the people. On the other hand they will greatly weaken his Lordship's hands and embarass his Government, if they raise a cry of "religion in danger," when it is *not* really in danger. They may rest assured that the High Court can have no sinister intention against the religion of the people. It is its duty to do justice between man and man, and not to unduly favour one religion to the prejudice of another. The Judges are not religious Zealots. We have thought it proper to explain this fact, because a false religious cry would be a dangerous game. When our religion is really in danger, we should certainly have recourse to all lawful and constitutional means for its protection, but happily that is not now the question at issue. We should certainly fight out the grave public issues involved in the recent contempt case, but we fear we will injure our own cause, ff we divert our attention from them by an unfounded religious alarm."

It would not be fair on our part if we were to omit to mention that Kristo Das incurred some unpopularity for the first article which he wrote on the subject, and for not having had the courage to see Babu Surendranath personally in Jail as a brother journalist, and not attending the public meetings held to express sympathy for him. Although at heart he sympathized with Babu Surendranath he found himself in a position in which he could not act up to his convictions.

We conclude this chapter of Babu Kristo Das Pal's life with the following extract from his own writing about his journalistic career :—

"Our First Decade.—With the present issue the *Patriot* enters upon the eighteenth year of its existence. Our connection with it dates so far back as 1857, but the last year completed the first decade of our editorial management of it In conducting it our sole aim has been the good of our country thorough good report and evil report, and how far our humble labors have tended towards that object we leave it to our readers and the public at large to judge If we have succeeded to any appreciable extent, however slight, we claim no credit for ourselves, but attribute the success, whatever it is, entirely to the merits of the great cause, which we have espoused, and to which we have devoted ourselves we may say from our school-days. We cannot, however, be too grateful to our numerous constituents, scattered through the length and breadth of the land, for the liberal patronage they have accorded to us. . . . If our brethern of the Native Press have often been found to fall in with our views and opinions, and if our educated countrymen sympathize with our sentiments and echo our utterances, it is because we think as they think, and in doing so we do not claim any leadership or "pre-eminence." If the nation chooses to make the *Patriot* its organ, we feel grateful to it, and we think that we will be able to serve it better by following the humble line we have chalked out than by aping the Frog in the fable to swell to the dimensions of the Bull—shall we say John Bull?"

CHAPTER V.

Career in the British Indian Asssociation.

Before we sketch out his career in this arena of political life, we think it right to make a passing allusion to the origin of this influential public body, which in days gone by rendered yeoman's service to the advancement of the political, and social condition of the people of this vast empire. It is proper to add at the outset that the British Indian Association was in fact a revival of the Landholders' Association started some years before, under the auspices of Babu Ram Gopal Ghose of immortal fame, and Baboo Joykishen Mookerjee, the public-spirited zemindar of Otterpara. The British Indian Association was first established on the 29th October 1851. From the first Annual Report of this Association, it appears that on the motion of Babu Nilmoney Muty Lal, seconded by Babu (now Dr.) Rajendra Lall Mitter the undermentioned gentlemen were appointed to be office-bearers for 1853 :—

Rajah Radhakant, *President.*
Rajah Kalikrishna, *Vice President.*

Rajah Suttochurn Ghosal,
Baboo Hurocoomar Tagore,
Baboo Prosonnocoomar Tagore,
Baboo Romanath Tagore,
Baboo Joykishen Mookerjee,
Baboo Aushootosh Dey,
Baboo Hureemohun Sen,
Baboo Ramgopaul Ghose,
Baboo Womesh Chunder Dutt,
Baboo Kishenkishore Ghose,
Baboo Jugudanund Mookerjee,
Baboo Pearychand Mittra, and
Sumbhoonath Pundit,
} *Members of the Committee.*

Baboo Debendernath Tagore, *Secretary* and
Baboo Degumber Mitter, *Assistant Secretary.*

In the same meeting the following Resolutions were adopted :—

On the motion of Rajah Kalikrishna, seconded by Babu Peary Chand Mittra :—

That Rajah Pertaup Chunder Singh be requested to accept the office of the Vice-President.

On the motion of Rajah Ishur Chunder Singh, seconded by Babu Hurish Chunder Mookerjee :—

That the Report of the Committee be printed in the English and vernacular languages, and circulated among the members of the Association and others.

As alluded to, in a previous chapter, Kristo Das was appointed Assistant Secretary to this great representative body of the Zemindars in 1858. The appointment of Assistant Secretary was formerly held by Babu Chandra Kumar Deb, and afterwards by Babu

Kally Prosunna Dutt, now one of the oldest vakeels of the Calcutta High Court. When the latter gentleman took up the practice of his profession, and vacated the post, Babu Huro Chundra Ghose took Kristo Das "by the hand" and used his influence to secure the appointment for his protege. Through his intercession with Rajah Radhakanta Deb Pahadur its President, and Rajah Protap Chunder Shing, and Maharajah Kali Krishen Bahadur, its Vice-President, and Rajah Ishur Chunder Shing its Secretary, Kristo Das succeeded in getting the appointment. *En passant* it may be remarked that, it was in the house of Raja Ishur Chunder Shing the Secretary, that Kristo Das became known to his great patron the Venerable Pundit Ishur Chundra Vidyasagur' who, as Kristo Das delighted to acknowledge to his intimate friends, had a great hand in his making. The new field of political life thus opened to him for the display of his great talents brought him in contact with Babus Hurish Chunder Mukerji, Ram Gopal Ghose, Sir Raja Radhakanta, Prosanna Kumar Tagore and Roma Nath Tagore, Babus Rajendra Lal Mittra and Digumber Mittra and others noted for their public spirit. Kristo turned to his advantage all the benefits derived from being associated with so many distinguished men. Human experience tells us that it is the circumstance that makes the man, and there is not the shadow of a doubt that, but for this highly favourable turn in his circumstance he would perhaps have never attained such high eminence. In this new field of great political activity, he worked with increasing success and distinction till at last he became not only the "Soul" of this public body, but also the virtual political leader in Bengal. Here he had opportunities to exhibit such rare qualities of statesmanship as, in any other country, would have brought him to the rank of a Palmerston and a Disraeli.

Scarcely three years had elapsed from the date of his joining the British Indian Association, when on the death of immortal Hurrish Chundra he was called upon to take up the editorial management of the *Hindoo Patriot*.

This was no small advantage to Kristo Das and the marvellous success which attended his career in the British Indian Association was partly due to this favourable circumstance.

Kristo Das used to say that he was greatly indebted to late Raja, Romanath Tagore for his rise in the British Indian Association. With the increase of his usefulness and influence his pay was gradually increased from Rs. 100 to Rs. 350 a month. In June 1879, he was appointed permanent Secretary.

To notice in minute details all his writings first as Assistant Secretary and then as Secretary to the Association is a subject for a volume, and cannot be compressed within the narrow space at our command. The British Indian Association being the only representative body, in days gone by, which sought to represent the wants, aspirations and grievances of the people, their task was indeed a herculean one. This gigantic task Kristo Das performed at the sacrifice of his life with great ability.

When any Mufusil civilian shewed any freaks or abused his power, Kristo Das was ready to use his pen for the vindication of the law and justice. Scarcely a year passed when it was not found necessary in the interest of the public to go up to Government with some sort of representations regarding the various legislative measures of successive imperial and local administrations. From the appointment of the famous Indigo Commission down to the enactment of the Rent Bill, all the important measures taken up by Government had to be criticized after great scrutiny, and this task Kristo Das performed with an ability which placed him in the front ranks of the Indian publicists. All the petitions, memorials, letters that had been written for the British Indian Association were the fruit of his intellectual labour. No doubt in drafting these memorials, he received much valuable assistance from his learned colleagues but it is undeniable that they were the productions of his own fertile brain.

We shall, however, close this chapter by noticing some of the important memorials submitted to Government by the British Indian Association.

In 1877 a memorial was submitted to the Viceroy

against the Provincial Public Works Cess Bill from which we make the following extract :—

"That Your Memorialists naturally feel diffident in carrying on controversy on a question, which the local Representative of Her Imperial Majesty holds has been closed by Her Majesty's Government. But they respectfully submit that, speaking on behalf of the vast population interested in land in these provinces, they occupy a peculiar position. They approach the Government holding a conflicting capacity ; firstly as one of the contracting parties to the covenant of the Permanent Settlement, on which they rely against any addition to the "State demand" upon the land ; and secondly as the arbiter, protector and guardian of the people. If they are denied a hearing by Government on the assumption that the question of the construction of the covenant of the Permanent Settlement has been closed by the imposition of the Road Cess (Act X of 1871 B.C.) and that it cannot be permitted to be opened when a new cess, quite dissimilar in scope, character, and mode of administration, is sought to be laid upon the land, they can only state that they will consider it their great misfortune. But whatever decision Your Excellency may arrive at on the subject, Your Memorialists are confident that Your Excellency will do so after giving a full consideration to the representations of those who feel aggrieved by the proposed legislation."

"That Your Memorialists do not propose to enter

in detail into the arguments advanced by His Honor the Lieutenant-Governor in his reply to Your Memorialists dated the 3rd instant, inasmuch as the points raised by His Honor have been fully discussed in their memorial to him. His Honor seems to be of opinion, 1stly, that the terms of the Permanent Settlement do not exclude the imposition of future taxes upon the land in addition to the *jumma* or the present land-tax; 2ndly, that the arguments advanced against the proposed Public Works Cess had been advanced against the Road Cess, and set aside by the Secretary of State; and 3rdly, that the irrigation works and State Railways are works of local utility and that the charge for them ought to be borne by the provincial fund. All these points have been noticed at length in the memorial of the Association referred to above, and your Memorialists will therefore briefly advert to them in this representation."

"That Your Memorialists deeply regret that His Honor the Lieutenant-Governor considers a respectful representation of their honest convictions as to the bearing of the proposed Cess upon the covenant of the Permanent Settlement as an "odious charge" against the Government. They submit with the utmost deference that it is the cherished privilege of the subject to lay his complaint before the sovereign, and if any act of the sovereign's representative should lead to what the subject humbly thinks involves a violation of a pledge of the sovereign, Your

Memorialists venture to think that the subject would not be true to himself and his sovereign, if he failed to bring his conscientious convictions and sentiments to the notice of the ruling power, which is the fountain of justice, and the source of redress of all grievances. Your Memorialists need hardly urge that the covenant of the Permanent Settlement was originally ratified by Parliament and the Crown, and that when the Government of India was transferred from the East India Company to the Crown Her Gracious Majesty the Queen and Empress was pleased to declare in Her Royal Proclamation, justly regarded as the Magna Charta of the people of India, that all treaties, engagements, and stipulations made by the Company's Government should be maintained inviolate."

The Memorial was followed by another submitted to the Secretary of State for India from which we extract the following with a view to shew with what a comprehensive grasp of the Permanent Settlement Question, Kristo Das wrote all these Memorials in a masterly way :—

"That if the necessities of the State should require the imposition of additional taxation, Your Memorialists are willing in all loyalty to bear their legitimate share in common with the rest of the community, but they pray that such taxation may be based on an equitable and impartial principle."

"That if it be argued that the "public demand" upon the land being fixed " for ever," the proprietors of land are best able to bear additional burdens, Your Memorialists take leave to dispute the correctness of that argument. In the first place it needs be borne in mind that the immediate effect of the Permanent Settlement was the destruction of most of the great families, which owned the land, in consequence of the crushing assessment under the Permanent Settlement and that if some of the original proprietors have lately improved their position, they have done so at considerable outlay of capital, and after years of toil, trouble and loss. In the second place that the vast majority of the proprietors at the present day have invested their capital at the market rate in perfect confidence in the promise contained in the Proclamation of the Permanent Settlement. It is well known that at the date of the settlement one-third of Bengal was covered with jungle, and it was the zemindars, who by giving advance to ryots, charging no rent or small rent for years, constructing embankments, excavating tanks, wells and channels, settling rent free-lands upon village establishment, and in other ways, reclaimed the land and rendered it productive. In the third place irrespective of the land-tax the holders of land have to pay most of the local taxes raised in Bengal, *viz.*, the Zemindari Dawk Cess, the Embankment Cess, the Municipal taxes, the Chowkidari tax, the Rural Police Cess, and the Road Cess. Such being the case Your Memorialists cannot perceive the justice of throwing the whole burden of the proposed addtional taxation upon the land alone throughout the province, when the benefits of the works, for which it is required, are confined to a few localities, in violation of the terms of the Permanent Settlement."

"Further, when the Permanent Settlement was concluded, it was done on the distinct understanding that the serious loss, which it inflicted upon the proprietors, would be compensated by future improvement, and if some proprietors have of years benefitted by the perpetual limitation of the state demand upon the land, the benefits which they enjoy were guaranteed by a voluntary act of the State, dictated by the then exigencies of the State as well as by other important considerations, and to turn round now and to say that because certain benefits have been created by that act of the State, therefore the class which have derived those benefits should be made, by the levy of a special tax upon the land, to give up a portion of those benefits, would have the effect of making an addition to the public demand upon the land, which they were originally assured would never be enhanced."

"That Your Memorialists accordingly pray that Your Lordship will be pleased to take the above facts and circumstances into consideration and to disallow the Public Works Cess Act in exercise of the powers vested in Your Lordship by the Indian Councils' Act."

Next to Babu Hurish Chunder Mukerjea, Kristo

Das possessed a full knowledge of the question in all its bearings. Mr. Montrio, the "Father of the Calcutta Bar" used to say to his pupils in the course of his lectures that Hurishe's articles on the subject would do credit to an English jurist. The same remark holds good in the case of Babu Kristo Das. He was an authority on the subject.

Kristo Das told us privately that once he carried on a controversy with Mr. Robert Knight, who was then the Editor of the *Bombay Times*, on the subject in a manner which extorted admiration from him.

The zemindars of Bengal owe him a debt immense of endless gratitude for the advocacy of their cause for the last quarter of a century.

As we have not space for more extracts, we close this chapter with the following extracts from a memorial submitted to the Viceroy in 1872 on "High Education in Bengal" :—

"If the abolition of the Mofussil Colleges has originated from a notion that the number of candidates who appear or pass at the University Examinations is not sufficiently large, or in proportion to the cost of the colleges, your Memorialists venture to remark that the same result obtains more or less in the colleges of all civilized countries. Nowhere is collegiate education self-supporting. Everywhere it is the few who avail themselves of high education, and although their individual contributions are not at all proportionate to the expences of the institutions, still the outlay upon those institutions is regarded as a most profitable investment for the advancement of national welfare, particularly remembering that it is the few in all countries, who are the intellectual leaders of the many. The State, your Memorialists humbly conceive, discharges its obligation to the people, when it places within the reach of all who may desire to avail themselves of the advantages of high education, means for such education, and if a few only among them come forward to participate in its benefits, that circumstance ought not to lead to the closing of colleges in a country when collegiate education has but just commenced, but to the adoption of measures to render them more easily accessible. It cannot be denied that the existing number of colleges in Bengal is not at all adequate to the wants of a large community scattered over so vast an area, and its reduction cannot fail to be regarded as a decidedly retrograde step."

"Your Memorialists take this opportunity also to draw the attention of your Excellency in Council, to the very unsatisfactory relation which subsists between the Government of Bengal, the Education Department, and the Calcutta University. The University has, after mature deliberation and consultation with the heads of all the colleges and principal schools of the country, laid down certain standards for general and especial education, and the Education

Department, until recently, very judiciously so regulated the courses of study in Government schools and colleges as to meet the requirements of the University. But His Honor the Lieutenant-Governor has lately set aside some of those courses, and ordered others which are calculated in a great measure to remove the schools and colleges from the healthy influence of the University. The abolition of the Urdu language, the restrictions on the study of Sanskrit, the new rules regarding scholarships, the introduction of special subjects as part of compulsory general instruction, are a few of the changes to which your Memorialists beg particularly to refer. It would be foreign to the object of this Memorial to enter into any enquiry as to the merits of these changes, but your Memorialists cannot refrain from observing that diversity of action and want of concord in the head of Government and the University authorities, cannot but prove prejudicial to the interests of education. Education is a subject in which grave differences of opinion must prevail in different individuals, and yet it is a plant of such slow growth that its fruit cannot be ascertained until after a long time. It is for the University, therefore, which represents the highest knowledge and experience of the subject in the country, to regulate and control its course and give it such firmness and stability as to ensure success. Sudden and frequent changes in its culture are liable to serious mischief."

" Your Memorialists cannot lay too much stress

upon the importance of certainty and definiteness in the policy of the Government in matters of administration. In this country, where the personel of Government changes every five years, there is naturally but too great temptation for the chief executive to signalize his administration by some conspicuous measures, and to distance, if possible, his predecessors; but this innovating tendency, unless tempered by discretion and controlled by the Supreme Government, is apt to give a rude shock to the cherished ideas and traditions of the people, to create alarm, distrust and unrest among them, and to disturb harmony in the different springs of action. It is not given to an Indian administrator to reap what he sows within the usual span of his official life. If, therefore, one rejects the plant planted by another and introduces new variety after his own fancy there can be no healthy growth, no sound development, no legitimate fruition. Fortunately for the cause of education, the leading principles have been laid down in the Hon'ble the Court of Directors' Despatch of 1854, which, as your Excellency in your recent address at the Medical College of Calcutta justly remarked, constitutes the Education Charter for India, but your Memorialists are grieved to submit, as they have ventured to point out, that those principles have been on several essential points widely departed from in the recent measures of the Bengal Government in the department of Education. If your Excellency in Council will condescend to examine the reasons, character and tendency of those measures, your Memorialists feel confident, your Excellency will be satisfied that the interference of the controlling authority of the Supreme Government is urgently needed."

CHAPTER VI.

Career in the Calcutta Municipality.

It was in 1863 that Babu Kristo Das was first appointed a Justice of the Peace and Municipal Commissioner of the Calcutta Municipality. In those days when the scheme of Local Self-Government was a thing unknown in the land, he was selected to take part in the deliberations of the corporate body in which the late Babu Ramgopal Ghose, the Hon'ble Romanath Tagore, Prosunna Kumar Tagore and Digumber Mitter, figured most conspicuously. Thus it was no small honour done to Kristo Das by the Government of the time to be early associated with such men of ability, rank and patriotism. He was then only on the thresh-hold of his future career of eminence and his selection therefore caused jealousy and heart-burnings in many a quarter. It is related that the grumbling on the occasion was such that Kristo Das needed consolation at the time, and Babu Sumbhu Chandra Mukerji consoled him by saying that the stamp of genius being on him, he had been selected by the Government more for his intrinsic worth than for any other consideration; and that the time would come when his enemies and detractors would see the justice of the selection. The prophecy was fulfilled to the very letter. Within the course of five or six years, the poor man of Kansaripara became the leading member of the Calcutta Municipality.

From his first appointment in the year 1863 down to the middle of the same year nothing can be known of his Municipal career for want of authentic information. In those days of darkness, proceedings of the Calcutta Municipality were not even allowed to be reported as it will appear later on, in the history of this great man. It was not till March 1864, that the proceedings of the Calcutta Corporation were allowed to be published in the Calcutta papers. From the abstract proceedings of a meeting held on the 17th August 1863, presided over by the then Chairman Mr. V. A. Schalch, it appears that when a resolution on the advisability of advertizing the time of every Meeting in the daily papers was put and lost, it was resolved on the motion of Maharaja Joteendra Mohun Tagore (seconded by Baboo Kristo Das Pal) :—

"That a list of the business to be brought forward before an ordinary Meeting should be hung up at the office of the Justices, at least two days previous to such Meetings."

It would thus appear that from the very beginning Babu Kristo Das felt the importance of giving publicity to the debates of the Council, in order to make the institution a popular one. It would not be out of place to mention here, that the first time, when the proceedings of the Calcutta Municipality were first made known to the public was the memorable day of the 21st March 1864." At a meeting held on that day, it was proposed by Babu Ramanath Tagore, perhaps according to the advice of Hon'ble Kristo Das Pal, that the "abstract proceedings of the Municipal Committee be sent to the daily and other papers of Calcutta." It was from this memorable day, the proceedings of the Calcutta Corporation saw the light of the day ; for this boon, the public are indebted to Mr. Roberts, Babu Ramanath Tagore, and Babu Kristo Das Pal.

The Water-Supply Question.

The next question of importance which engaged the attention of Babu Kristo Das Pal was the new water-supply scheme. It was prepared by Mr. Clarke, a distinguished Engineer and was estimated to cost nearly sixty lacs of Rupees, with an annual expenditure of six lacs. The scheme would necessitate the imposition of a water-rate upon the gross rental of all houses, buildings and lands within the town, and Kristo Das was opposed to it from the beginning on the ground that it was enormously expensive, that it was not adapted to the condition and habits of the bulk of the inhabitants and was calculated to interfere with their cherished religious convictions and feelings. He was of opinion—an opinion which was shared by Babu Degumber Mitra and Babu Romanath Tagore—that an ample supply of good drinking water could be provided at a far less cost by digging a number of tanks in the town. Before considering the merits or demerits of the question, it is better to relate here how it was opened. At a meeting held on the 6th February 1865, the Chairman (Mr. Schalch) moved the following resolution :—

"The Justices concurring in the opinion expressed by the Water-Supply and Finance Committees adopt the scheme which has been prepared by the Engineer for the supply of the Town of Calcutta with water and authorize the Chairman, subject to the sanction of His Honour the Lieutenant-Governor of Bengal under Section 33 of Act VI of 1863, to carry out the scheme in accordance with the recommendations of the above named Committee."

The Resolution was seconded by Mr. Howell, but Babu Kristo Das moved an amendment, seconded by Babu Romanath Tagore :—"That the consideration of the subject be adjourned to the first Meeting to be held in March." The Resolution with the amendment being put to the vote, was lost. Why Kristo Das wanted to put off the discussion to another meeting will appear from the following extract from his own writing on the subject in a pamphlet published under the heading "Remarks on the water-supply for Calcutta and dedicated to the Committee of the British Indian Association in 1855." He says :—"The Association in their letter to Government complained that a scheme of such a gigantic magnitude was adopted by the Justices without discussion, notwithstanding a motion for adjournment. That motion was made by me, but the Chairman of the Justices remarked that it was quite open to the opponents of the scheme to have expressed their objections to its adoption and to have invited discussion as to its merits. I stated at the meeting that the Report of the Engineer had been circulated among the Justices only two days previous to the meeting, and that they had not consequently sufficient time to study it. I for one was then not prepared to discuss the subject, for it could by no means be expected that one could decide off hand at two day's notice a subject which it must have taken the Engineer and the Chairman weeks, if not months, to digest. And would it have signified much if the subject had been postponed for a fort-night or a month in order to give the Justices due time to mature their opinion upon it? Besides, the wording of the notice of the Chairman, so far as I understood it, did not indicate that the subject would be finally disposed of at the meeting of the 6th February. The notice thus ran:—"The Chairman to lay on the table Mr. Clark's scheme for supplying the Town of Calcutta with water, having Pultah as the source of supply with the recommendations of the Drainage and Water-Supply Committees." It was not added that the Chairman would move the adoption of the Report. Remembering that the Chairman had not long ago enunciated his course in respect of important matters to be, that papers should be laid on the table at the one meeting and should be discussed at the next, I naturally concluded that the Report of the Engineer would not be adopted at the meeting of the 6th February. This was also the impression of my friends who supported my motion. But we were taken by surprise when the Chairman moved for the adoption of the Report with the recommendations of the Water-Supply and Finance Committees, burdening the Town with a fresh charge of 6 lacs per annum, and consequently leading to additional taxation equal to nearly 50 per cent of the present Municipal income. Hence I deemed it my duty to call for adjournment, but my motion was negatived."

In this pamphlet he discussed the water-supply question at elaborate length. The limited space at our command does not allow us to make extracts from his writings on this subject.

We are convinced that the opposition offered to this scheme of water-supply by the Hon'ble Kristo Das Pal arose from his honest conviction that it would be ruinously expensive to the people.

As regards his apprehension that the Hindoos would not use pipe-water, it might be said that being a rigid Hindu himself, he shared the popular impression of the time which he afterwards abandoned as an erroneous one.

Whenever this question came to be discussed by the Municipal Commissioners, Kristo Das never failed to represent public grievances connected with it.

The Municipal Market Question.

The proposal of establishing a Municipal market for the benefit of the Europeans residing in the town in close proximity to the Dhurumtola Market was first considered by the Municipality in 1866, and had to be abandoned for want of funds and other reasons. Sir Stuart Hogg who succeeded Mr. Schalch in 1866, took the side of the Europeans and exerted his whole influence from time to time to get this market established. Whenever the question happened to be discussed Kristo Das opposed it with all the oratorical display of powers of a great debator. We have not space here to notice in minute detail all these speeches delivered by him on this important question. Suffice it to say that it was through his influence that an amicable settlement was come to, between the late Babu Muty Lal Seal the proprietor of the Dhurumtola market and Sir Stuart Hogg in regard to the establishment of the Municipal market.

Stipendiary Magistrateship for the disposal of Municipal cases.

From the proceedings of a meeting held on the 13th September 1866, it appears that Sir Stuart Hogg then chairman of the Municipality moved a resolution :—

"That Babu Kristo Das Pal be appointed for six months on a salary of Rs. 300 per mensem for trying Municipal cases."

Raja Romanath Tagore seconded the above resolution. Mr. Roberts having suggested that Government be applied to for a stipendiary Magistrate, the motion of the Chairman was lost. Even if this appointment had been conferred upon Babu Kristo Das, he could not have accepted it without compromising himself in the eyes of the public. He never aspired for Government service as he felt that God had marked him out for a higher distinction than it was in the power of any temporal power to bestow. In this connection it may be mentioned that once Sir William Grey wanted to offer him the appointment of the Vice-Chairman of the Calcutta Municipality which he declined. Conscious of his superior ability he chose to work in his own line and in fullness of time highest glory attended his successful career.

Lord Ulick Browne as Chairman.

In March 1872 Lord Ulick Browne was appointed as Chairman of the Calcutta Municipality and held the appointment only for ten months; and it was during this short time that Lord Ulick proposed various measures which were hotly opposed by four gentlemen of the Calcutta Municipality *viz.*, Mr. J. B. Roberts, Mr. F. F. Wyman, Dr. Rajendra Lal Mitter and Babu Kristo Das Pal who were then known under the sobriquet of "the quartetto." We have no desire to judge harshly of the conduct of Lord Ulick towards these four gentlemen who did their best to protect the interests of the rate-payers of the town. But we cannot help mentioning one or two instances in which the chairman sought to curb the independence of these gentlemen. Once he took it into his head to issue a circular appointing a miscellaneous committee of 24 Justices regarding which it would be better on our part to speak in the words of the *Englishman* newspaper. It says :—

"The tendency of this move (appointment of Miscellaneous Committee) is evidently to remove all practical control over municipal affairs further than ever from the general body of the Justices. An examination of the list of Justices proposed for this Committee will show that they are almost without exception men who are known to be constant supporters of the Chairman. But few of the Justices whom we are accustomed to look to for independent action, are included in it. If there be any necessity for such a Committee as that proposed, it evidently ought to be so constituted as fairly to represent all parties."

The *Friend of India* wrote as follows on the same subject :—

"The reference to Baboo Kristo Das Pal is very much worse, because there is no instance in which this gentleman has taken up a position at all like one of antagonism to the Chairman. We have never seen a speech of his in which gibes, or personalities, formed any part. As a writer there is no calmer or more cautious in India, and there are questions which he has so thoroughly made his own that he has a right to deal with them with an authority that no other journalist in India possesses, while, if a question of style arose, his writing would be pronounced good English where Lord Ulick Browne's if it came under the adjudication of a schoolmaster would run a great risk of the treatment which schoolmasters award in cases of language badly constructed, dreadfully involved, and utterly wanting in courtesies and amenities of life."

Then again the Chairman sought to restrict the time for which a speaker at the Municipal Board could address his audience to 15 minutes, and the *Englishman* remarked as follows :—

"We view the rejection of the motion (fifteen minutes rule) with satisfaction, because it was obviously directed against one particular Justice,—a fact which the Chairman himself was careful to place beyond doubt by his reference to the remarks on the subject that appeared lately in the columns of a contemporary. Taken in connection with this reference, and with what had passed at a previous meeting regarding the matter, we consider that the motion was most offensive and objectionable."

The Calcutta native public expressed their confidence in these gentlemen and disapproved of the conduct of the Chairman.

The Outram Statue.

The following story which we have heard from Babu Nilmoney Mookerjee, Sanskrit Professor, Presidency College, to whom Kristo Das related it in the course of a private conversation will serve to shew that, when opportunity presented itself, Kristo Das was too willing to lend his help to a righteous and sacred cause. Sir James Outram's statue which now adorns the Maidan, stood in need of ornamental gas-lamps, and they were supplied through the help of the Hon'ble Kristo Das Pal. The help rendered in this cause may have been trifling, but it is none the less valuable when viewed in the light it deserves.

On the 23rd May 1874, Lord Napier of Magdala, the Commander-in-Chief unveiled the above statue in the presence of Lord Northbrook, then Viceroy of India. The Committee of the Outram statue requested the Municipal authorities of Calcutta to put ornamental gas-lamps round the enclosure. The proposal was first mooted in the Town Council held on the 13th April 1874 and the following Resolution was adopted :—

"That as the statue stands on the Maidan, and not within the town of Calcutta, the Committee is not prepared to recommend the Justices to contribute towards the erection of ornamental gas-lamps, or to defray any of the cost of lighting the same."

Lord Napier who was on the Outram Committee, we believe, requested Babu Kristo Das privately to get the order of the Town Council reversed and to make the Municipality pay for fitting up ornamental lamps. He accordingly at the General Meeting held on the 11th May 1874, moved the following Resolution :—

"That the application of the Outram Committee be complied with, and that six lamps be provided to light the Chowringhee side of the Outram enclosure, it being understood that the lamps on the Maidan side be set up by the Outram Committee."

The Resolution was seconded by Mr. R. Harvey and carried by a large majority, though some of the members both European and native were opposed to it.

The Calcutta Municipal Bill of 1876.

Kristo Das opposed the passing of this Bill which sought to confer upon the people the right of electing their own representatives in the Municipal Committee. For this precious boon the people of Calcutta are indebted to Sir Richard Temple then Lieutenant-Governor of Bengal. What were the grounds of his opposition to this Bill will be apparent from the following extract from his writing :—

Firstly.—Because the Bill, though it professes to concede self-government to the people of Calcutta, leaves the appointment and dismissal of the Chief Executive Officer in the hands of Government, and thus destroys one of the most essential characteristics of self-goverment.

Secondly.—Because the Bill sanctions the union

of the functions of Chairman of the Commissioners and Commissioner of Police in the hands of one person, which is detrimental to efficiency, tends to divide responsibility, and opens a door to abuse of power. This centralization of authority is not required in the interest of the town, inasmuch as the experience gained in the sister capitals of Madras and Bombay shews that the separation of the two offices works there smoothy and satisfactorily.

Thirdly.—Because the Bill sanctions additional objects for municipal expenditure, which, though optional, may be enforced at the discretion of the Commissioners, and which, when enforced, are likely to result in additional taxation. The multiplication of municipal expenditure on objects of secondary importance, when the town is burdened with a heavy debt, and its primary requirements cannot be satisfactorily met with from want of funds, is much to be regretted.

Fourthly.—Because the Bill reduces the hours of the supply of water at high pressure from 17 to 3 during twenty-four hours, though it enhances the the water-rate from 5 to 6 per cent. The reduction of the water-supply will place the people at considerable disadvantage and imperil the success of the drainage system.

In an article headed "A Temple of Fame" he criticised Sir Richard's policy thus :—

"Calcutta has been in the possession of the English more or less directly since they came to trade in the East, but what governor had had the moral courage magnanimity, or sincere love of the people to concede to them the glorious privilege of municipal self-Government, the inestimable boon of the franchise, and the unsurpassable honor of sitting in solemn conclave in the civic corporation of the town ? And yet they are ungrateful enough not to appreciate this privilege, this boon, this honor. They have the audacity to look the gift horse in the mouth, and because it does not suit their fancy they spurn at it. Could there be blacker ingratitude than this ? But the Governor is a loving father of the people. He sees that his children do not understand him, do not realize the profuse paternal affection he cherishes for them, and yet he is over-flowing with kindness to them."

"People blame Sir Stuart Hogg, but we do not do so because we know that his fault has been, if we may call it a fault, that he has been too loyal to Government ? And what could he do ? He is a servant of Government and its representative in the corporation and how could he go against the views and wishes of Government ? He himself said at a meeting of the Justices that he was willing to take in Mr. Roberts as his deputy, if the Justices should so wish, but it should be remembered that there was the pressure from above, and he could not resist it. As regards the Municipal Constitution none knows better than he that it would be an unmitigated sham; he has said so in private as well as in public; he declared his opinion in open Council, but if the Government insisted upon it he could not help it. He justly holds that if a "lower class of society are to be brought to govern the town, they cannot be trusted with plenary powers, that in that case he must keep the power in his own hands, veiled through the Government, and that it is for the Government to square its account with the public as to how far the scheme proposed is calculated to satisfy their reasonable wishes and aspirations. If the Municipal Bill will keep away men, to whose counsel he would willingly bow, whose co-operation he would gladly seek, and whose support he would readily take, it is not his fault. It is Sir Richard Temple, who is solely and primarily responsible for the measure. And what is his excuse ? He cannot say that the present system has *per se* broken down ; if it has broken down, that has been entirely owing to the under hand manipulations of Government. If the Government had allowed the corporation fair play, if it had not sought to override the independent Justices by putting official pressure upon the frail and fragile portion of the tribe ; if it had not sought to swamp them by appointing new men " between whom and the Government there was a community of sentiment and feeling," the existing system would not have broken down. And now that the Government has helped in breaking down the present Corporation, it is essaying to replace it by a constitution, which public opinion unanimously declares will be a greater sham than the present."

" We have said above that we wonder at the attitude Sir Richard Temple has assumed towards the Calcutta public, and we are lost in wonder. In his fondness for his pet measure he seems to have forgotten the usual amenities of public life. A most influential deputation of the British Indian Association waited upon His Honor on Thursday last to present the memorial adopted at the meeting of the rate-payers. It comprised the principal rate-payers of the town, who we may say own three-fourths of it. They have a most momentous stake in it, and they have been naturally moved to their innermost depths by the proposed measure. And what was the treatment they received at the hands of the Lieutenant-Governor? They had forwarded a copy of the memorial three days previous, but the Lieutenant-Governor had no specific reply to make. We have seen many deputations to the Governor-General and the Lieutenant-Governor, and read accounts of similar deputations to ministers in England, but we have never seen a single deputation, the spokesman of which was made to stand for nearly an hour while all others including the great man upon whom they waited were sitting, and cross-questioned while standing without being favoured with a formal reply. But this was exactly what Sir Richard Temple did. If he did not intend to give a formal reply, though this was an unusual course, we do not understand why he made Babu Degumber Mitter read the memorial or why he cross-examined him upon points, which had been fully set forth in it. The Lieutenant-Governor asked the deputation what would they want, if the Government could not give an elective system under the conditions they had urged, and they at once replied that they would rather have a continuance of the present system than one which would be a greater farce. But if His Honor had read the memorial, he would have been saved the trouble of putting this question. Strange to say that while the Lieutenant-Governor chatted about the different sections the amendment of which was prayed for in the memorial and invited the opinion of the deputation, His Honor did not condescend to express his own opinion upon a single question of principle. He evaded the questions of the union of functions of the Chairman of the Justices and Commissioner of Police, of the regulation of Police expenditure, of water-supply, of bustee improvement and the like."

Kristo Das from his seat in the Bengal Council made a long speech on the Bill from which we make the following extract :—

"The Hon'ble Baboo Kristo Das Pal said a *quondam* Governor General of India, alike distinguished for ability and eloquence, once remarked that the Legislative Council of India was a standing committee of changes. If proof was wanted to illustrate the truth of that saying, the history of municipal legislation of Calcutta afforded a notable proof. The first law which gave the present constitution to the Calcutta Municipality was passed in 1863, and within the last twelve years about twelve Acts, including those for markets, had been enacted, giving on an average one Municipal Act for the town per annum. Thus there were changes almost annually going on in the municipal law of Calcutta. The time had arrived for the consolidation of those laws, and the task could not have been undertaken by a worthier individual than his hon'ble friend in charge of the Bill. He had had experience of the working of the Municipality for the last nine years, and his energy and ability had always extorted the admiration of the community and the Government, though there had been occasional differences of opinion between the Justices and himself regarding his method of action. The present Bill aimed at the consolidation of ten Acts, excluding the market Acts. The hon'ble mover had said that the question of the incorporation of the Market Acts might be considered in the Select Committee, who might, if they should think proper, include them in the Bill. For his own part, he thought that the law relating to the Municipality of Calcutta should be one, and that the Market Acts should not be left separate: but the Select Committee would doubtless consider that important point. The hon'ble mover of the Bill had explained that he had not touched the constitution of the corporation; but the hon'ble member to his right (Mr. Schalch) had suggested that the present opportunity should be taken to improve the constitution, if practicable. The hon'ble gentleman was the first to inaugurate the present municipal system of Calcutta, and he had considerable experience in the working of it. He was now the head of another Corporation, which, though limited in its scope, had still very important and somewhat analogous functions to perform; and occupying the vantage ground he did as the head of that Corporation, he saw the defects that disfigured the neighbouring institution."

"If a move was to be made for the amendment of the municipal constitution of Calcutta, he hoped that that the right of election on a broad basis would be conceded. He was not prepared to say that the Council was in a position, or that the time had arrived, to concede a thorough elective system to the town of Calcutta; but he must observe that no mere tinkering of the municipal constitution would satisfy the public. If it was thought advisable to give the citizens of Calcutta the right of self-government, they ought to have it fully and unreservedly. But then the question would arise—suppose the elective system be conceded, should the Chairman be elected by the representatives of the town, or should his appointment rest with the Government? Now there could be no thorough elective system unless the Chairman's appointment were also made elective; and with the question of the appointment of the Chairman arose many important questions which it was not desirable to discuss here. He was of opinion that for a long time to come it would not be desirable to separate the appointment of the Chairman of the Justices from the Civil Service. He had seen the working of the Calcutta Municipality for the last twelve years, and he must confess that, though the proceedings of the Chairman might have been sometimes characterized by an arbitrary spirit, he had proved an honest administrator of public funds and public affairs. There could not be a more trustworthy agent than a member of the Civil Service. If, then, the Council were not prepared to leave the election of the Chairman in the hands of the town Council, would it be worth its while to constitute a Corporation, composed partly of members nominated by the existing Corporation, partly of delegates from the public Associations of Calcutta, and partly of members appointed by the Government? Now with regard to the Associations of Calcutta, although he had the honour to belong to one of them, he must admit that they were not permanent bodies, and it was therefore open to question as to whether the permanent interests of the town should be committed to bodies who lived on the breath of their subscribers. In the next place the hon'ble member proposed that the Town Council should be formed on the model of the Port Commission, and that its proceedings should be conducted in the manner of those of the Port Commissioners. Now, with every deference to the Port Commissioners, he hoped the Council would not pass any measures which would reduce the Town Corporation to the level of the Port Commission."

"It would be presumptuous on his part to remind the Council that in those civilized countries where the privilege of the elective franchise was enjoyed, the right of nominating the executive officer who administered the municipality was not claimed by the Government. Of course, the position of India was somewhat peculiar, and the experiment of self-government was also new. But the experience gained in the Presidency of Bombay ought to be a fair guide to us in Calcutta. If the people of Calcutta did not fall short of their brethern in Bombay in intelligence and public spirit, he did not see why the people of Calcutta should be treated in different manner from those of Bombay."

He thus pointed out the necessity of separating the function of the Chairman and Commissioner of Police :—

"Then the proposition he had embodied in these sections contemplated another material change. He meant the separation of the offices of Chairman of the Justices and Commissioner of Police. And here he might inform the Council that he was not aware of any civilized city where the chief of the police was the chief of the Municipality. It was not so in civilized Europe as far as he was aware; he believed it was not so in America; and it was not so even in the capitals of Bombay and Madras. If, then, in the sister capitals of Bombay and Madras it had been found quite practicable to carry on the municipal government without uniting the functions of Chairman of the Municipal Corporation and Commissioner of Police in one person, he saw no reason whatever for centralizing authority in the hands of one executive officer in this town. The practical effect of this centralization was divided responsibility."

The Bill was passed in 1876 notwithstanding the opposition of the Hon'ble Kristo Das Pal. He fought most strenuously for the privilege of electing the Chairman, but he was defeated in Council. Several material alterations were, however, made in the Bill at his suggestion.

Sir Stuart Hogg's retirement.

When Sir Stuart Hogg took 23 months leave from the 13th November 1876 the Hon'ble Kristo Das made the following speech :—

"He did not think Sir Stuart Hogg regretted his connection with the Municipality. He was comparatively junior member of the Service when in the Mofusil, but since he had been in Calcutta he had attained to the position of a prominent member of the Service. Within six months of his connection with the Municipality the Justices marked their confidence in him by raising his allowance to Rs. 3500 and he believed he owed the privilege of wearing his Knight sword to his connection with the Municipality, as in his position he had the honour of welcoming two princes of the Blood-royal to the Metropolis of India. While he acknowledged the eminent services of their worthy Chairman he was ready to admit that there were suns spots and black spots in his escutcheon. But, on the whole they could not find a more able devoted conscientious and fearless public servant than he was."

At a meeting held in 1878 when the Chairman submitted a resolution passed by the Town Council on a letter from Sir Stuart Hogg, resigning his appointment as Chairman of the Commissioners, the Hon'ble Kristo Das Pal moved " that the Resolution of the Town Council be adopted, and that a copy of it be sent to Sir Stuart Hogg."

In moving the Resolution he made the following speech :—

"Although he did not claim seniority in years to over many of the Commissioners, he was the oldest member of the Corporation. He was a member of the old Corporation from its establishment, and had therefore opportunities of observing the Municipality under several able, experienced gentlemen who had from time to time presided over the municipal affairs of the town; and he was in a position to state that Sir Stuart Hogg yielded to none in ability, zeal and energy in the performance of the many onerous duties as Head of the Corporation of the Metropolis of British India. There had been many passages-at-arms between what he called the independent Justices and Sir Stuart Hogg; but notwithstanding all their differences, he was glad to be able to say that they understood each other, and that although Sir Stuart Hogg was sometimes led away by impulse and given to excessive expenditure in several matters against the wishes and opinions of his independent colleagues, his administration, on the whole, was successful and creditable to him. He never cherished any personal ill-feelings against his opponents; and if Baboo Kristo Das Pal were permitted, he could shew the Commissioners a letter which he had received a mail or two ago from Sir Stuart Hogg, in which he had the candour to state that though they were fierce opponents in the Municipal debates, they always respected each other and entertained a warm feeling for each other. He was not only an energetic Chairman but our energetic citizen as well. The Commissioners might remember the rush of famine population in Calcutta in 1869. Who took the lead in drawing schemes for their relief; in building famine camps, and attending to the wants of those unfortunate men and women ? Then came the visit of the Duke of Edinburgh to the city. His Royal Highness visited the town in 1869. On whom did the arrangement for giving a fitting reception to him devolve ? It was Sir Stuart Hogg."

"In the same way it became his duty to organize arrangements for the reception of the Prince of Wales, when, as on all public occasions in which the town had to be represented, Sir Stuart Hogg, as Chief of the Corporation, took a leading and active part. For all the services he had rendered to the town as Head* of the Corporation and as an active citizen representing the Corporation and the town on all public matters he thought his services deserved recognition from this body; and although the Commissioners did not then exist as members of this Corporation, as rate-payers they should record the sense they entertained for services he rendered them."

The motion was seconded by Mr. R. Mitter and unanimously adopted.

Memorial for Mr. Souttar.

The Hon'ble Kristo Das was ever ready to shew his respect to those distinguished Civilians who had held the appointment of Chairman of the Municipality. He made the following speech on the above subject :—

"The Hon'ble Kristo Das Pal said, that he rose with a heavy heart to move the Resolution which stood in his name, and as few words were needed to commend it to the approval of the Commissioners he would be brief. The lamented deceased was well known to all the Commissioners, and it is not therefore necessary to go to any length to describe to them what sort of a man he was and what were the services he rendered to the Municipality. In November 1878 Mr. Souttar was appointed to fill the Chair which their present Chairman holds. He had previously distinguished himself as an administrator in controlling affairs of the Suburban Municipality, and in connection with the work he did there, he believed that he came under the favorable notice of the Lieutenant-Governor. When His Honor selected Mr.

Souttar to fill the most important Municipal Office in the Bengal Province, he believed His Honor had special regard to the success with which Mr. Souttar had administered the affairs of the Suburban Municipality. He would ask them to look back to the time when he joined this Corporation. Its funds were low, its credit was low, it was threatened with a serious deficit, and it required a vigorous effort of retrenchment and economy to make the two ends meet. The Budget Committee was then about to sit to consider the financial situation of the Municipality, and it was at such a time that Mr. Souttar assumed charge of his office. He at once agreed with the Budget Committee that, without extensive retrenchments, it would not be possible to restore equilibrium between income and expenditure, and so he heartily co-operated with them in reducing expenditure. It was true the desired equilibrium was not restored by mere economy; the Commissioners were obliged to have recourse to the maximum rate of taxation, but when that was done, the two ends were brought together, and there was a fair prospect before them for the next year. Mr. Souttar resolutely carried out the policy of economy, and at the end of the following year, the Commissioners were able to reduce taxation. He did not hesitate to say that, without the hearty co-operation of Mr. Souttar it would not have been possible to restore the equilibrium of the finance. His friend Baboo Kally Nath Mitter reminded him that when the draft Budget for

1879 was laid before the Budget Committee, as it was prepared by his predecessor, the Commissoners were threatened with a deficit of eight lakhs of rupees with the house-rate raised to the maximum of ten per cent. The situation was then most perplexing. It might as well be said that the Municipality was threatened with bankruptcy. But as they already said, with the hearty co-operation of Mr. Souttar, they were able to tide over the crisis which then threatened to overwhelm them. From the day he took charge Mr. Souttar resolved to enforce the strictest economy, and he loyally carried-out the resolutions of the Commissioners. With regard to all matters of finance and admininstration Mr. Souttar was a loyal adherent to law; he was staunch to the Municipal Constitution, and the speaker did not remember that he did a single thing by which he attempted to override the law or the constitution or the deliberate resolutions of the Commissioners. He would always take the Commissioners into his confidence, and the Commissioners in return reposed the utmost confidence in him. He meant no disparagement when he said that the Civil Service represents a powerful bureaucracy which rules the land, but those gentlemen who come here have a very difficult task to perform; they have to face the representatives of the peoples in the great task of Municipal self-government. And their difficulties were not a little aggravated by the fact that this Corporation represented the varied elements of great community of this city. Mr. Souttar was fully alive to the difficulties of his position, but he was a warm advocate of the elective system, and one of his last acts in the administration of the Municipality was to leave on record in the last Administration Report the opinion that, as far as he could see, the elective system had proved a great success in Calcutta, and that if the Commissioners should continue to act with judgment, care and foresight even worst enemies would not be able to find fault with them."

Such was the tribute of respect paid by Kristo Das to the memory of Mr. Souttar.

The Contagious Diseases Act.

At a meeting held in August 1882, Kristo Das made the following pathetic appeal against it when the Chairman submitted for confirmation, the following Resolution passed on the 11th July :—

"That as the Contagious Diseases Act is now worked solely for the protection of soldiers and sailors, and as the Lock Hospital is virtually monopolised by women registered under the Act, the Municipality ought not to be called upon to contribute towards its support."

He thus spoke :—

"As for the general question it had been already argued out so ably that it was unnecessary for him to say anything further. The sense of the native community from the very inception of the law had been against it. The Act was introduced into this country under the auspices of Lord Lawrence and Sir Henry Maine. The object was chiefly to protect soldiers and sailors but it was thought advisable to extend it to the civil population to see whether it would work beneficially or not. But the moral feelings of native population had been all along arrayed against it. The native community, while regretting the evils which prevailed, had always maintained that there was a sense of modesty even amongst fallen women which ought not to be outraged. They were not taken, for there had been many a sad end to life among the poor unfortunates in order to escape the horrors of the Act. It was not desirable therefore to extend or to encourage any measure which would extend the operation of the Act to the native population. The Government had thoroughly considered this question; a very influential Committee was appointed, presided over by no less an authority than the Commander-in-Chief, and in that Committee the town was represented by the Deputy Commissioner of Police, Mr. Lambert. And that Committee came to the conclusion that the operation of this law should not be extended to the civil population, but only to the parts of Calcutta frequented by soldiers and sailors. When the civil population was exempted from the operation of the law, the Government had no right to call upon the Municipality representing that population to contribute. It was neither fair nor just that, for the sake of a few immoral and diseased women, who availed themselves of the benefit of the hospital, the whole of the rate-payers should be compelled to pay. It, would be a tribute to vice, and the sooner the Commissioners freed themselves from this tribute the better."

The Deficiency in the Water-Supply.

In 1884, four months previous to his death, Kristo Das protested vehemently against the deficiency in the Water-Supply in an elaborate speech from which we make the following extract :—

"The Hon'ble Kristo Das Pal said that he found it was at an unfortunate moment he gave notice of his motion on the subject, for the subject should have been discussed that day fortnight, so that it seemed it was at an unfortunate moment that he took up the subject. Nevertheless, he must go through his task. At the last Meeting owing to the hurricane which raged, the matter was put off, and if it had not been for the reasonableness of the Chairman, he did not know whether the subject could have been brought before the Meeting till that day, three months, to which date that Meeting was adjourned. The subject of his motion was now uppermost in the thoughts of all the inhabitants of the town of Calcutta There was not a part of the town in which the cry for water was not heard, and he was obliged to confess that, with that cry, imprecations were hurled at the heads of the Municipal Commissioners of the town. The rate-payers complained that thay paid the full rate demanded from them, but that they did not get the quantity of water they were entitled to, and they asked why, under such circumstances, they should be expected to pay the full rate. The question of deficient water supply was not new; it had been pressed upon the attention of the Commissioners from the time when the water supply was first provided for the town; because if the speaker recollected rightly, it was in 1871 that Mr. Clark was called upon to consider the question of doubling the supply, though at that time, the want was not so imminent. For the last five years the question of double supply had presented itself, and the Commissioners had been active and zealous in discussing it. It was sometimes said that the Commissioners lost a great deal of time in considering the question, and were, therefore, retarding the extension, the want of which they now felt so much. The speaker did not agree with those who thought that they lost too much time in deliberating over the matter."

Thus it would appear that from the very beginning of his career, he never lost an opportunity of representing public grievances in the matter.

The Municipal career of Babu Kristo Das Pal extending over a quarter of a century was a most successful and brilliant one. He first took his seat in the civic corporation as a nominee of Government, but he ever followed the dictates of his conscience in protecting the interests of the rate-payers of the town. He was the chief adviser of Government and its civilian representatives in all important matters and his influence over many of them was indeed very great. In fact, he was one of the most active, useful and influential members of the Corporation. We close this chapter of his life with the following extract from the *Indian Mirror* of the 26th July 1884 in which its Editor Babu Norendra Nath Sen thus alluded to his Municipal career :—

"Being then recognised as among the leading men of the Native community, it was natural that he should have been selected a member of the then new body of Justices, to whom the administration of the Municipal affairs of Calcutta was entrusted in suppression of the old triumvirate. Here, again, a new erana was thrown open for the display of those oratorical powers for which he deservedly enjoyed so high a reputation. His readiness at reply and the force and fluency of his language and his extensive knowledge of the condition of the city always secured him a willing audience. His powers were shown to such uncommon advantage in the discussions on the questions of the new Municipal Market that his reputation which was then in some measure confined among his own community, soon began to spread among European circles. Without doubt, he was the most prominent member of the Calcutta Municipality, and it is only a fitting mark of respect to his memory that the Municipal Office was closed for business for a day.' So complete was the ascendency he had at one time established over the Municipal Board, that no action in any important matter was taken by it without his advice. Every successive Chairman felt and acknowledged in his proceedings that Kristo Das Pal was the life and soul of the Municipality. To his influence many men, now in the Municipal service, owe their original appointment and subsequent advancement."

CHAPTER VII.

HIS LEGISLATIVE CAREER.

Kristo Das having achieved great success first as a journalist and then as a Municipal Commissioner of the Calcutta Corporation, it was natural to expect that he should be called upon by the Government to help it in the task of legislating for the country. In 1872 he was appointed a Member of the Bengal Legislative Council. As a Member of the Bengal Council he took part in the discussions of every Legislative measure taken up by Government for the good administration of this country. In discharging this onerous public duty he had to make considerable sacrifices of his time, and the strain on his intellectual labour was considerably increased. He displayed his marvellous talents in discussing questions of vital importance to the people of Bengal. For instance in 1873 when the Hon'ble Mr. Dampier moved for the consolidation and amendment of the Mofussil Municipalities Bill, Kristo Das made an elaborate speech thereon which considerably enhanced his reputation both in the eyes of the public and the Government. He advocated the interests of the Mofussil Municipalities and the law was shaped and much modified according to his many valuable suggestions. Then again when the Hon'ble Mr. Schalch moved for the amendment of the Court of Wards' Act of 1870 Kristo Das made very valuable suggestions in connection with it.

His speech on the Provincial Public Works Cess Bill is a master piece of its kind. For want of space we cannot make any extracts from these speeches. He brought to bear upon the discussions of these questions that came before the Legislative Council the vast information he possessed regarding the economic and the social condition of the people and never failed to point out any shortcomings that he found, so far as the interests of the country were concerned. Although he lent his support to the Government in the task of legislation he never shirked the duty of criticizing its conduct when occasions arose. From Sir George Campbell down to Sir Ashley Eden every successive Lieutenant Governor of Bengal acknowledged publicly the invaluable services rendered by him as a Member of the Bengal Council.

We now come to consider his career as an Additional Member of the Imperial Legislative Council.

On the 9th February 1883 he first took his seat therein as the representative of the Bengal zemindars in the discussion on the Rent Bill which was then under the consideration of the Governor-General in Council. The discussion turned upon the intricate problem of the Permanent Settlement question, and Kristo Das defended the zemindars and advocated their cause in a way for which the zemindars will ever remain grateful to him.

The Criminal Procedure Code Amendment Bill.

Before we come to consider this part of his Legislative career, we shall have to allude to the part played by Babu Kristo Das Pal in the controversy on the Ilbert Bill question. Since the outbreak of the Mutiny the tension of feeling between the Europeans and Natives was never so great as during this time. It was during this most excitable time that Kristo Das advocated the interests of his fellow-countrymen in a most calm and moderate spirit. The following speeches will corroborate the fact that from his seat in the Council, he performed the most difficult task of assuaging the rancorous hostile feelings of the Anglo-Indians in a truly patriotic way. At a meeting of the Legislative Council held on the 9th March 1883 when the Hon'ble Mr. Ilbert moved for the publication of the Bill together with the statement of its objects and reasons, Kristo Das made the following speech :—

"My Lord,—I think I would best consult the the interests of the Bill if I should say as little as possible on the subject. I am convinced that I cannot do better than leave it to your Lordship, as the responsible head of the Government, to enunciate the reasons and policy of this measure. I cannot, however, allow this occasion to pass without saying that I look upon this Bill as a legitimate and logical development of the progressive policy which characterises British rule in this country, and that, its principle being sound, just and righteous, my countrymen feel a deep interest in it."

"None, my Lord, can regret more than I do the ebullition of feeling which this Bill has caused. Considering the innocuous character of the Bill, I confess I did not expect it, nor did the Government, I believe, anticipate it. Had it not been for the great important principle at stake, I would have been the first to counsel the withdrawal of the Bill, rather than oppose the wave of feeling which has risen against it. I have too strong a faith in the character of John Bull to believe for a moment that he will carry to the bitter end his opposition to a noble attempt to establish that equality in the eye of the law which the history of his own country, and the teachings of his own political system, so loudly proclaim. I was young when the hurricane of the Sepoy Revolt burst over the country in 1857, but I well recollect how feelings were torn asunder by the sad events of those days, how furious was the rage of denunciation, and how terrible the voice of vengeance. And yet, when the storm of the Mutiny subsided, the feeling also subsided, and not a few of those who had stood forth as uncompromising enemies of the Natives now stepped forward as zealous champions of their cause. It has been my good fortune to work with many of them, and to profit not a little by their advice, assistance, co-operation and example. Who could for a moment say that the Anglo-Indian of the Mutiny days was the Anglo-Indian of the succeeding days of peace and progress? This is my experience of the character of honest John Bull."

"Pride of race—I use the phrase in no offensive sonse—is a commendable feeling. It is an honest and honourable pride. It has been the mother of good deeds, valiant acts, patriotic exertions and national glory. But there is a higher and nobler pride, that of fostering human happiness under beneficent law, raising the week and lowly to the level of the strong and high, and making equal law and equal justice the basis of political paramountcy in the world. It is to that noble feeling I appeal. All Englishmen, whether in India or in England, I humbly think, should rejoice that, within the century and a quarter they have ruled India, they have effected such a complete revolution in the Indian mind, both intellectual and moral, that Indian Magistrates are found fit to be trusted with the administration of the laws of the land, not only over their own countrymen, but also over the members of the ruling race. This is a work of which England may justly feel proud—this is a consummation over which all Englishmen may well rejoice."

On the 4th January 1884, Kristo Das made the following speech when the Bill was referred to the Select Committee and when the Government entered into a *concordat* with the Anglo-Indian community :—

"My Lord, I approach this subject with a mingled feeling of satisfaction and sorrow—satisfaction because the settlement referred to concludes 'a message of peace with a body of gentlemen who, however misguided and maddened on the present occasion, are undoubtedly important factors in the cause of the advancement and regeneration of this country, and sorrow because, unless carefully safeguarded, it may open a wide door to injustice. I love peace, but honour more, and justice above all. It is not my object to dwell on the history of the present scheme of legislation, on the bitter feelings and animosities which it has evoked, on the gradual minimization of the effect of the Bill, small by degrees and beautifully less, or on the influence which the angry discussions of the past ten months may have on the political prospects of the people. I say—let bye-gones be bye-gones. My present concern is to consider how far the proposed settlement will secure the interests and ends of justice. The primary object of your Lordship's Government in the proposed legislation has been to wipe out the brand of race-disqualification in the judiciary within certain limits in the trial of European British subjects. And that object, I am happy to observe, has been steadily kept in view, and for it our grateful thanks are due to your Excellency's Government. I must at the same time confess that the scope of the original Bill, itself a small measure, has been materially reduced by the modifications proposed from time to time. As far as I understand these modifications, both the Native and European Sessions Judges and the Native and European District Magistrates will be so far placed on a footing of equality that they will exercise equal jurisdictiox over European British subjects in matters criminal. This equalization, however, has been attained not by extension, but by reduction, of power; by taking away the power of independent action of European Magistrates, and not by adding to the power of Native Magistrates. In so far, I am constrained to say, the solution of the difficulty has been achieved by an unsatisfactory process. The anomaly of race-distinction is doubtless removed as between Magistrates, but it is effected not by adding to the power of Native Magistrates, but by changing the *venu*. Race-distinction becomes most obtrusive only in the trial of a certain class of cases, and those cases are practically transferred from the file of the Native Magistrate to that of his juniors the Joint-Magistrate."

On the 25th January 1884, Kristo Das thus dwelt

on the desirability of extending the system of Jury-trial to the natives of the country :—

"Bearing in mind what fell from your Lordship the other day, deprecating the raising of the general question of extension of jury-trial for Natives, I thought it proper not to bring forward any amendment or motion on the subject. I would have remained silent if my hon'ble friend the Maharaja of Durbhanga had not brought forward his motion. The subject, however, being mooted in Council, I consider it my duty to support the motion. I need not remind hon'ble members of Council that, in a country where the panchayat system has been in force from time immemorial, trial by jury cannot be said to be an exotic. The people are familiar with the institution, and although it has prevailed here, under a different name, its practical working has been the same here as in more civilized countries. It is unnecessary for me to dwell on the well known advantages of the jury-system, but it is not from any sentimental considerations or a regard for tradition that I support the institution. I do hold that jury-trial is really the bulwark of the liberty of the subject, and that it is a material safeguard of the interests of justice. How the jury-system has been working in Bengal is, I believe, well known to the hon'ble members of this Council. I am well aware that many executive officers are not much in favour of trial by jury, but we should not forget that not a few of them are apt to push their vigour beyond the law. The question lately came, I observe, before the Lieutenant-Governor of Bengal in connection with the police administration report, and I will, with the permission of the Council, read an extract from the Resolution of His Honour showing how essential is the jury-system to the interests of justice, even if thereby now and then miscarriages of justice occur. His Honour remarks :—

"The unwillingness of juries to convict in serious cases involving the issues of life and death may sometimes have been the cause of failures of justice, which would not have occured had the person been tried by a Judge and assessors. What is now complained of is not, it must be remembered, a new thing. It has been a charge against the system of trial by jury from the first ; but it by no means follows that the unsatisfactory results in the trial of murder-cases by jury is solely owing to the willingness of the jurors to convict in a case in which a capital sentence would probably be passed. It is in the experience of the Lieutenant-Governor that jurors look with much greater strictness into the evidence and to the conduct of the police-officers than unassisted Judges used to do ; and it is much better that it should be so, notwithstanding occasional failures of justice. The over-scrupulousness of juries, if such it may be called, should have its effect on the action of the police and upon the investigations made in Magistrate's Courts, with results which can be only beneficial.'

"Such is the opinion of the responsible head of the Bengal Government, and I believe that all right-minded men who value jury-trial will come to the same conclusion. In fact, I look upon the jury-system as a most useful instrument of self-culture and self-discipline in the administration of the affairs of a nation. It has, however, been urged that all parts of the country are not equally ripe for jury-trial, and that, therefore, the time has not yet arrived for the universal extension of the system to the country. Now, my reply is, that when the wilds of Assam have been declared to be fit for jury-trial, there can scarcely be any part of the country in Bengal, Northern India, Madras or Bombay which cannot be said to be sufficiently advanced for the reception of this boon. I am quite aware that there may be backward parts where jury-trial would not be an unmixed blessing, but as civilization is progressing and education is advancing the people of those districts will gradually acquire that knowledge and experience which will enable them to enjoy the privilege without injury. Then it is contended that, as the motion involves what I may call a big change, it ought not to be passed without reference to the Local Governments. I confess I do not look upon the motion in that light. It is true that it contemplates a material change by converting assessor-districts into jury-districts, but, as I have already said, if the Government of Assam could extend the jury-system to all the territories under it, I do not see why this

Council, knowing the position of the different provisions, cannot extend the system of jury-trial to the whole country without further reference to the Local Governments. I go further. I submit that the Bill before us introduces large and radical changes into the system of jury-trial as regards European British subjects; that is to say, it gives European British subjects the right to claim a trial by Jury before a District Magistrate, which they had never before enjoyed, and yet it has been considered unnecessary to refer the matter to the Local Governments for opinion. So if, in introducing such a big change in respect to the trial of European British subjects, it has not been considered necessary to consult the Local Governments, surely this Council can consistently take action in this matter without reference to Local Governments. I think it is due to the Maharaja to point out that his motion does not at all affect the agreement or arrangement made with regard to the trial of European British subjects. As far as I understand him, he leaves that question where it is, and does not wish to interfere with or disturb the arrangement made. He simply asks that the Indian subject tried in a Sessions Court should have the privilege of demanding a jury just as the European British subject would be entitled to do. In this respect he claims an equality between the European and the Native which I do not think will be considered unreasonable. In fact, from what has fallen from the previous speakers, I perceive that their sympathy is with the motion, though they consider that the present time is not quite opportune for pressing it. Then it may be said that this motion does not come quite within the scope of the Bill because it does not form part of the arrangement made with the opponents of the measure. Now, the hon'ble and learned mover of the Bill has already pointed out that the Select Committee had admitted certain amendments which were outside the agreement. In the same spirit this matter may be entertained, though it is outside the agreement. The object of the motion, as I take it, is to improve the administration of justice, and surely whatever may tend to improve the administration of justice deserves the consideration of the Council. How the administration of justice will be improved I think the extract which I have just read from the Resolution of the Lieutenant-Governor clearly explains. I hold that the present motion is quite consistent with the scope of the Bill before us, firstly, because it aims at the establishment of an equality in the eye of the law between the different classes of Her Majesty's subjects, which has been the primary object of the Bill, and secondly, because it is a proposal for the improved administration of justice, which, I submit, is also one of the objects of the Bill."

Kristo Das made the following speech just before the final passing of the Bill :—

"My Lord, before the motion is formally put to

the vote, I ask your Lordship's permission to say a few words. I feel it would be wrong on my part to raise a fresh discussion upon a subject which has been already discussed threadbare, particularly as the Bill has reached the stage when no discussion will avail one way or another. Remembering also the deliberate decision of Government that the Bill must be based on the lines of the agreement entered into, I could see no room for any substantial amendment which would prove beneficial, and I am confirmed in my opinion by the proceedings of this day. At the same time, in justice to myself, I must candidly confess with due deference that the provisions of the Bill as amended by the Select Committee, as far as I can see, are not calculated to remove the apprehensions which I ventured to express on the last occasion. It cannot be denied that while race-distinction is removed in one direction, that is to say, as regards a very small class of Native 'officers, it is deepened in another direction, that is to say, as regards the Native population at large, that the anomaly of jury-trial in petty cases, in cases in which a jury is admitted to be ridiculous, remains all the same, if the District Magistrate chooses to try such cases; that the cure of the invidiousness of the law will depend on the forbearance of the Magistrate, if he will not try petty cases, and of the accused, if he will not claim a jury in such cases; that the risk of failure of justice at the hands of a dominant and sympathising jury is not safeguarded in any way, and that the old evils to poor complainants of the transfer of cases to distant Courts, almost amounting to a denial of justice, from districts where a jury may not be available, will be revived in all their rigours. But I will not prolong a dying controversy by raising fresh objections. Your Lordship was pleased to declare, in winding up the debate on the 7th instant, that a failure of justice such as I had apprehended would be an intolerable evil, that if your Lordship had anticipated it, you would not have been a party to be arrangement made, and that should failure of justice or other grave evils hereafter arise out of the proposed system, it would be the duty of the Government of the day to apply adequate remedies. I accept this assurance of your Lordship with due submission."

"My Lord, if I have correctly gauged the opinion of my countrymen on this subject, there seems to be a deep conviction among them that the fiery ordeal through which they have passed during the last ten months has brought forth no adequate result that if they have gained some slight advantages on the one hand, they have lost much more on the other, that the sudden and sad turn which this business has taken at the last moment has fallen like a thunderbolt upon them, and filled them with gloom and dismay. But I should not despond. The main principles of this Bill, though within very narrow limits, being affirmed, I fervently hope that it will prove the precursor of more substantial and abiding reforms. At some favourable time hereafter, when the present storm of passionate feelings and race-animosities, it is to be hoped, will have passed away, when practical experience will have satisfied even the most thorough-going representatives of the domineering class that Native Judges and Magistrates mete out even-handed and uncoloured justice, some hopeful mariner in charge of the vessel of the State, following the signal planted to-day, may steer his course in the same onward path, and give a wider effect to the high hopes and honourable aspirations with which the controversy of the past few months, I am bound to say, has filled the heart of the nation."

The Bengal Tenancy Bill.

The Zemindars of Bengal and Behar were greatly alarmed by this legislative scare-crow and great was the agitation they set up in connexion with it. They went up to Government with a request to allow them the privilege of hearing them by proxy. Agreeably with this request Lord Ripon allowed the British Indian Association to nominate a member to the Legislative Council to take part in the deliberations on this question which affected the rights of the landlords of Bengal and Behar. Kristo Das was unanimously nominated to be their spokesman in the Council. At a meeting held on 12th March 1883, he made an opening speech on this subject from which we transcribe the following :—

"I wish to begin with a personal explanation, for

which I crave your Lordship's indulgence. It may be supposed that, as I have the honour to sit in this Council under your Lordship's orders, with the suffrage of the landholders, it is my duty to look to the interests of the landholders alone. But such is not the case. I cannot divest myself of my natural sympathy with the millions who till the soil and constitute the back-bone of the nation. Indeed, I would not be true to myself, to my cherished convictions, and to my humble labours for the promotion of my country's welfare, if I were to shut my eyes to the interests of one party for the sake of the other. All that I want is justice and fair play to both. No good landlord, I submit, my Lord, is blind to the interests and happiness of his tenantry. In fact, rightly, understood, the interests of the two are interwoven with those of each other. A prosperous and contented tenantry is a blessing to the landlord and to the country at large. In considering the vitally important question before us, happily we have not to deal with a *tabulâ rasa,* and are not left to our own unaided judgment. Both the landlord and tenant in Bengal have their charter of rights, and if we rightly interpret that charter we cannot go far wrong."

For want of space we cannot extract anything more from his long speech on this subject.

CHAPTER VIII.

HIS DEATH AND CHARACTER.

. We have already said that overwork and want of rest made Kristo Das Pal subject to an attack of Diabetes in 1872. Although he partially recovered from the disease, through the treatment of a native physician, his general health quite broke down and from time to time, specially in the hot weather, he was found ailing. To regain his health and to enjoy a little rest so far as was consistent with the urgent nature of his duties, he once went to Kotechandpore in the District of Jessore with Babu Protap Chunder Ghose and then again to the Busirhat sub-division with his friend Babu Kader Nath Dutt.

Previous to his death he went to ⋅ live at a garden-house at Kamargachee belonging to Babu Brindabun Chunder Bose, in company with his friends Dr. Rajendra Lal Mitter, and Professor Nilmoney Mookerjee. He was in the habit of taking morning baths in the Ganges and exposure to cold brought on fever which he could not shake off and which ultimately put an end to his life so precious to his countrymen on the 24th July 1884. He suffered the most excruciating pains for nearly three months with an almost superhuman patience and resignation. Babu Prosad Das Dutt of Jorasanko his most intimate friend relates to us that eight days previous to his death it was suggested by his friends to try a change of treatment and to put him under Dr. Mahendra Lal Sircar, M. D., the eminent Homœopathic physician of Calcutta. Kristo Das knew that his case was hopeless aud change of treatment would not benefit him. He therefore said that at that stage of his illness he was most reluctant to throw the odium of failure on his intimate friend Dr. Sircar. Such was his kind thoughtfulness and large sympathetic nature even in the throes of death.

Kristo Das was fully prepared to meet death in a cool and courageous way. He knew from a long time past that the nature of his work would not allow him that amount of rest which the doctors thought in his case to be indispensable for the prolongation of his life, and that the disease which was lurking in his system might kill him at no distant date Working all along under this belief he managed, by practising the utmost economy, to make ample provision for his parents, his widow and children and for other helpless relatives whom he had left behind him. Before his death he executed a Will from which we extract the following :—

"This is the last Will and Testament of Sree Kristo Das Pal, of 108 Baranushee Ghoshe's Street, in the town of Calcutta, a Hindoo gentleman.

I hereby revoke all former Wills and other Testamentary dispositions and writings made by me at any time or times heretofore, and do publish this to be my last Will and Testament in the manner and form following (that is to say) I nominate and appoint Prosad Das Dutt and Kedar Nath Dutt, both of No. 1, Sikdarpara Lane, of Calcutta and my son Radha Churn Pal, executors of this my Will.

I direct that the Executors shall pay the legacies mentioned hereunder—

1st My father Rs. 10,000 (ten thousand).
2nd ,, mother ,, 10,000   Ditto
3rd ,, daughter ,, 10,000   Ditto
4th ,, wife   ,, 10,000   Ditto.
5th ,, cousin   ,,   500 (five hundred).
6th ,, female relation who attends on my mother Rs. 200 (two hundred).
7th The District Charitable Society of Calcutta Rs. 10,000 (ten thousands).

to be invested in Government Securities, the interest of which is to be applied by the native committee of the Society to the maintenance or education of indigent Hindu students by giving them a monthly stipend not exceeding Rs. 3 per head per month.

I direct and empower the said Executors to manage my estate that shall come to their hands with absolute power and also to sell, mortgage, contract, transfer and alienate and to collect and to realize the rents, profits, interests of the whole or any part thereof; and that the receipt or receipts of the Executors shall be sufficient discharge for the sale, mortgage or alienation to the person or persons paying the same. In witness whereof, I, the said Kristo Das Pal have to this my Will set my hand, the 9th day of July in the Christian year 1884.

Signed, published, declared and acknowledged by the said Kristo Das Pal as and for his last Will and Testament in the presence of us and in the presence of each other, and we have hereunto subscribed our name as witness.

MAHENDRA NARAIN DAS,
PROTAP CHANDRA GHOSE,
The 9th July 1884.

KRISTO DAS PAL.

Having dwelt in previous chapters on his public character, we shall complete the history of his life by saying something on his private character. Kristo Das was no less esteemed for his private virtues than for his public character. He was simple in his taste and abstemious in his habits. Nurtured in the lap of cold adversity he, when fortune smiled upon him did not forget the lessons of his past life. He had no idea of luxury and even when he rose to the proud distinction of being a member of the Legislative Council he was seen to go there in a *ticca gharry* or in a *palanquin.* Such was the simplicity of his character, that he was very often seen dressed as plainly as any one. He cherished a deep respect towards his parents, and at their bidding he celebrated many a times the expensive Durga Pujah in his house. Affectionate as he was to his children and his family, he was no less kind to his neighbours and others. Busy as he was, he gladly assisted many a helpless men by drafting petitions for them. The call on his time for like gratuitous work was indeed very great. Hosts of people came from various quarters with various requests; some came for petition, some for advice and some for recommendatory notes for employment. From early dawn till midnight, Kristo Das was seen in his room surrounded by crowds of these people and doing their business with an ungrudging spirit. We can testify to the fact that as a master of methodical work and possessing a marvellous memory he could write long articles for the *Hindoo Patriot* on difficult subjects, and at the same time carry on conversation with a number of people. Those who had come to see him generally went away greatly impressed with the sweetness of his temper and courtesy. In holding conversation with those present, he made no distinction and was very careful to say something to every one. Once we took a friend to Kristo Das and introduced him by saying that he had come to make his acquaintance. He was a poor village school-master. Kristo Das had a long conversation with him on paddy, the village police and such other topics as only a villager could take an interest in. This reminded us of what Sir Walter Scott had done while travelling in a Railway carriage to have a talk with a shoemaker.

In helping the poor and the friendless he had to make considerable sacrifices of time and forego many comforts of domestic life. Even during his illness he never neglected to help those who sought his help. It is related of him that once an up-countryman came to him to get a petition drafted. Kristo Das was then in a garden-house and there the poor man went at night-fall. Although the friends of Kristo Das hesitated at first on the ground of his ill-health to allow this man to get an interview with him, this poor man managed to see him personally and the petition was drawn up for him that very night.

Kristo Das was the most popular man in Calcutta, and he gained that popularity by an uniform sweetness of disposition towards all manner of men. He never spoke harshly even when he was overworked to death. His temper was as serene as his balance of mind perfect. This was the secret of his popularity. It is no exaggeration to say that in this great town he had very few enemies if any at all. He was loved by all and respected by many. His death is a serious loss to the country. We have no desire here to dwell upon that melancholy subject at any length.

On his death, all the public bodies of India and almost all the leading men both European and native expressed sympathy with the bereaved family. For want of space we extract only two letters on the subject :—

FROM LORD NORTHBROOK,
Late Viceroy and Governor-General of India.

MY DEAR MAHARAJAH,

I was very grieved to-day at the news of the death of Rai Bahadur Kristo Das Pal, and I should be greatly obliged to you if you would take an opportunity of assuring his relatives of my sincere sympathy.

The great ability of Kristo Das Pal, his remarkable knowledge of all questions relating to India, both in their Indian and English aspect, and the manner in which he conducted the *Hindoo Patriot*, made him undoubtedly one of the most distinguished of your fellow-countrymen.

I have read his journal constantly now for many years, and I have much appreciated not only the talent shown in its articles but the high tone and friendly spirit towards the Government in which current questions have been discussed.

I feel the loss of such a man in the midst of his career of usefulness is a national loss.

Believe me,
Yours very truly,
(Sd.) NORTHBROOK.

FROM SIR ASHLEY EDEN,
31st July, Carlstadt, Austria.

MY DEAR JOTENDRA,

I can't tell you how grieved and shocked I have

been to see the telegraphic announcement of the death of our friend Kristo Das.

I knew that he had been suffering for a long time past from that curse of your country, Diabetes; I had however no idea that he was in a critical condition. His loss to Bengal will be irreparable, for I know no man who can aspire to take his place as a thoughtful, moderate, earnest advocate of native rights. . . . . I can only hope that as Kristo Das was found to wear the mantle of Hurish Chunder, some one may be found to take the place of Kristo Das, but I doubt it.

Yours sincerely,
(Sd.) A. Eden.

To commemorate his life, a large public meeting was held on the 10th January 1885 under the presidentship of Sir Augustus Rivers Thompson, Lieutenant-Governor of Bengal. A committee was formed to raise subscriptions for the perpetuation of his memory in a suitable manner. It was suggested at the time that an Eye-Infirmary in his name should be established. Dr. Mahendra Lal Sircar suggested at the meeting that a marble statue should be erected. Although more than two years have elapsed since his death, the amount of subscription did not come up to more than Rs. 14,000. As is usual in this country, departed worth is not much appreciated and as yet no definite step has been taken to perpetuate his sacred memory.

APPENDIX.

The following copy of the Bengali Trust-Deed has been kindly placed at our disposal by Babu Prasad Das Dutt, the Executor and the Guardian of the minor son of Babu Kristo Das Pal.

টুষ্ট ডিড্

হিন্দুপেটিয়ট

শ্রীযুক্ত রাজা প্রতাপচন্দ্র সিংহ ও শ্রীযুক্ত বাবু রমানাথ ঠাকুর ও শ্রীযুক্ত বাবু যতীন্দ্রমোহন ঠাকুর ও শ্রীযুক্ত বাবু রাজেন্দ্রলাল মিত্র মহাশয়গণ বরাবরেষু।

"লিখিতং শ্রীকালীপ্রসন্ন সিংহ সাকিম কলিকাতা জোড়াসাঁকো টুষ্টি নামা পত্রমিদং কার্য্যানুক্রাগে আমি নানাবিধ বৈষয়িক কার্য্য মধ্যে সদা সর্ব্বদা আরত থাকায় হিন্দুপেটিয়ট্ নামক ইংরাজি সংবাদ পত্র সম্পূর্ণ রূপে দৃষ্টি করিয়া নির্ব্বাহ করায় অশক্ত বিধায় উক্ত সম্বাদ পত্র ও তৎসম্বন্ধীয় টাইপ অর্থাৎ অক্ষর মায় লওয়া জমা ও লহনা আদায়ের বিল প্রভৃতি আপনাদের হস্তে অর্পণ করিয়া আপনাদিগকে টুষ্টি নিযুক্ত করিলাম। আপনারা এই সম্বাদ পত্র ও অক্ষর ও পাওনা টাকা প্রভৃতির টুষ্টি সূত্রে মালিক হইয়া নীচের লিখিত নিয়ম প্রতিপালন পূর্ব্বক ঐ কাগজের সমুদায় কর্ম্ম সুচারুরূপে নির্ব্বাহ করিবেন। যেহেতু আপনাদিগের হস্তে ঐ ছাপার কাগজ থাকিলে দেশের নানাবিধ উপকার হইবার সম্ভাবনা। এমতে স্বীকার করিতেছি যে উক্ত কাগজের অক্ষর ও লওয়া জমা দ্রব্য ও উপস্বত্বের প্রতি আমার স্বত্ব রহিল না। কস্মিনকালে আমি কিম্বা আমার উত্তরাধিকারী কোন দাবী দাওয়া করিব না ও করিবেন না। যদি করি কিম্বা করেন, সে বাতিল ও না মঞ্জুর।

নিয়ম।

১। অত্র পেট্রিয়ট কাগজের গত এডিটার ৺ হরিশচন্দ্র মুখোপাধ্যায়ের নামে স্থায়ী থাকা জন্য এই হিন্দুপেট্রিয়ট নাম কখন পরিবর্ত্তন হইবে না। যে পর্য্যন্ত এই কাগজ আপনাদের হস্তে থাকিবে, তাবৎকাল ঐ কাগজের নাম হিন্দুপেট্রিয়ট নামে প্রচলিত থাকিবেক। এবং আপনারা ঐ কাগজ অন্য কোন সম্বাদ কাগজের সহিত যোগ কিম্বা মিশ্রিত করিতে পারিবেন না।

২। কম্মিনকালে এই হিন্দুপেট্রিয়টের কর্ম্ম নির্ব্বাহ কালে আপনাদের কর্তৃত্ব কালে কোন রকমে ক্ষতি হইতে পারিবে না। আর ঐ কাগজ ও তাহার গুড উইল ব্যতীত তৎ সম্বন্ধীয় অক্ষর আর লওয়া জমা বিক্রয় করিতে আপনাদের ক্ষমতা থাকিবে। কিন্তু ঐ মূল্যের টাকা আপনারা নিজে ভোগ না করিয়া প্রেসের দেনা শোধ বাদ আর অবশিষ্ট টাকা হরিশ মেমোরিয়াল ফাণ্ডে অর্পণ করিবেন।

৩। অন্য কোন কাগজ পেট্রিয়টের সহিত মিশ্রিত করিলে কিম্বা আপনারা স্বয়ং কোন মুদ্রা যন্ত্রালয় প্রভৃতি ক্রয় করিয়া পেট্রিয়টের কাগজের সহিত মিশ্রিত করিলে সেই কাগজের আপনাদিগের ক্রয় করা যন্ত্র কি অন্য পদার্থ আপনাদিগের স্বেচ্ছানুসারে বিক্রয় করিলে তদুপস্বত্ব আপনাদিগের ইচ্ছা মত ব্যয় করিবেন।

৪। হিন্দুপেট্রিয়ট কাগজের কর্ম্ম চালাইবার আয় ব্যয়ের হিসাবাদি আপনাদিগের নিকটে আমার লইবার ক্ষমতা রহিল না।

৫। হিন্দুপেট্রিয়ট কাগজ ও তাহার গুড উইল বিক্রয় করার ক্ষমতা রহিল না। ঐ কাগজ মায় গুড উইল দেশের উপকারার্থে কেহ প্রার্থনা করেন তাহা উপযুক্ত বিবেচনা করিয়া দান করিতে পারিবেন।

৬। আপনাদিগের কাহারও কোন লোকান্তর হইলে কিম্বা কেহ আপনার ইচ্ছা পূর্ব্বক টুষ্টির ভার পরিত্যাগ করিলে যাঁহারা উপস্থিত থাকিবেন তাঁহারা ইচ্ছামত পরিত্যাগ কিম্বা মৃত টুষ্টির পরিবর্ত্তে তত্তুল্য ক্ষমতাবান অন্য টুষ্টি নিযুক্ত করিতে পারিবেন।

৭। টুষ্টির সংখ্যা তিন জনের কম ও পাঁচ জনের অধিক হইবে না ও টুষ্টি নিয়োগের নিমিত্ত আমার মতের প্রয়োজন হইবেক না

TRUST-DEED. 179

ও আমি আপনাদিগের পরিবর্ত্তে কখন অন্য ট্রষ্টি নিযুক্ত ও আপনাদিগকে রহিত করিতে পারিব না।

৮। আপনারা ঐক্য হইয়া সর্ব্বদা ট্রষ্টি কর্ম্ম নির্ব্বাহ করিবেন। আপনাদিগের মধ্যে মতের অনৈক্য হইলে অধিকাংশ ট্রষ্টির যেরূপ অভিপ্রায় হইবে সেই মত কার্য্য নির্ব্বাহ হইবেক।

৯। যদি কোন ট্রষ্টি ইনসল্ভেণ্ট হয়েন কিম্বা কোন রকমে অকর্ম্মণ্য হয়েন অথবা অন্য কোন অপকর্ম্ম করেন তবে তাঁহাকে বহিষ্কৃত করিয়া তাঁহার স্থানে আপনারা অন্য ট্রষ্টি নিযুক্ত করিতে পারিবেন।

১০। এই ট্রষ্টি নির্ব্বাহ করিবার নিমিত্ত আমি একজন ট্রষ্টি আপনাদিগের সহিত থাকিলাম। এবং আপনাদিগের তুল্য ক্ষমতাপন্ন হইয়া ট্রষ্টির স্বরূপ উপরের লিখিত নিয়ম সকল প্রতিপালন করিব। যদি উপরের লিখিত নিয়ম সকল অন্যথা করি তবে নয় দফার সর্ত আপনারা আমার প্রতি খাটাইতে পারিবেন।

১১। উপরোক্ত নিয়ম সকল প্রতিপালন পূর্ব্বক হিন্দু পেট্রিয়টের কার্য্য নির্ব্বাহ হইবেক ও দুই দফায় লিখিত অনুসারে বিক্রয় করা আবশ্যক হইলে বিক্রয় হইবেক। এতদর্থে পেট্রিয়ট কাগজ ও অক্ষর মায় লওয়া জমা মালিকত্ব পরিত্যাগ করিয়া ট্রষ্টি নামা লিখিয়া দিলাম। ইতি সন ১২৬৯ সাল ৪ঠা শ্রাবণ।

কলিকাতা   শ্রীকালীপ্রসন্ন সিংহ
২৯ জুলাই ১৮৬২ সাল
        সাক্ষী
শ্রী নবীনচন্দ্র মুখোপাধ্যায়
শ্রী কৃষ্ণদাস পাল

Translation of the Trust-Deed of the Hindoo Patriot.

To
    Srijuta Raja Protap Chandra Shingha and Srijuta Babu Romanath Tagore and Srijuta Babu Jotindra Mohun Tagore and Srijuta Babu Rajendra Lal Mitter.

APPENDIX.

Written by Srijuta Kaliprasanna Shingha, of Calcutta Jorashanka, is this trust-deed.

Being always variously engaged, and being unable to fully supervise and conduct the work with regard to the *Hindoo Patriot*,—an English newspaper so named,—the said newspaper and the type, fittings, and furniture of the same, together with the power of realizing outstanding bills, &c., do I hereby make over to you and do hereby appoint you trustees of the same.

You, holding the newspaper and the type and the debts &c. as trustees, shall, in the following manner, following the undermentioned rules, conduct all business connected with and arising in the management of the paper, duly and satisfactorily ; as in your hands the paper will likely be of service to the country. I do hereby admit that henceforward I shall have no right or property or share in the returns of the same paper, type, furniture &c.

That at no subsequent time shall I, or my heirs, or assigns claim the same or hold the same to be subject to any claims. If I, or any of my heirs, assigns do set up such a claim it shall be null and void.

RULES.

(1). That, during the time of the late editor, the late Babu Hurrish Chunder Mukerjee,—this paper, the *Hindoo Patriot*, having been so named and established, the name *Hindoo Patriot* shall never be changed. That so long as the paper shall remain in your trust, the said paper shall be published under the name of the *Hindoo Patriot*, and that you shall not incorporate or amalgamate the same with any other newspaper or newspapers.

(2). That you shall, at no time, injure or prejudice the working of the same, during the period of your management. That moreover excepting the said newspaper and the good-will for the same you are hereby empowered to sell the type, fittings, and furniture of the same. But that you shall, without enjoying the money so realized by sale, pay out of the same the debts of the paper and make over the balance, if any, to the Hurrish Memorial Fund.

(3). If you amalgamate the *Hindoo Patriot* with any other newspaper, or if you incorporate with the same *Hindoo Patriot* any Printing Press &c., such press, types, fittings and furniture &c., you shall be at liberty to sell at your will, and employ the returns of the same in whatever manner you may please.

(4). That I shall have no power to call for the accounts or make you accountable for the receipts and disbursements as account of the same paper.

(5). That you shall have no right to sell the newspaper namely the *Hindoo Patriot*, or the good-will of the same. But you are hereby empowered to make over the said newspaper and the good-will of the same to any person or persons who may, in your judgment, seem fit and proper for the purpose of doing good to the country, and if they so apply.

(6). At the decease of any of you or if any of you withdraw from the trust, the surviving trustees may at their will resign or appoint in his place another trustee of like abilities and influence.

(7). That the number of trustees shall not exceed five nor be less than three. Nor shall it be necessary to consult me with reference to the appointment of trustees. I shall have no power to appoint other trustees in your place, or hinder you.

(8). That you shall conjointly and in agreement conduct the business. If there be any variance of opinion the paper shall be conducted according to the opinion of the majority.

(9). If any trustee be declared insolvent, or if he be in any way incapacitated or commit felony (or do a misdeed) you shall remove him and have the power to appoint a new trustee in his place.

(10). To do the trust duties I remain with you as a trustee and shall have like powers as yours and follow the abovementioned rules. If I conduct myself otherwise than as herein laid down, you shall have the power to carry out the requirements of para. nine of this deed.

(11). The abovementioned rules shall be followed in the working of the *Hindoo Patriot*, and further if as laid down in para. two it be necessary to sell, it shall be sold.

For these reasons I renounce all proprietary right and claim to the *Hindoo Patriot*, the type, fittings, and furniture &c.; and write this trust-deed—this the 4th of Sraban of 1269 Bengali year.

CALCUTTA: } (Sd.) SREE KALIPRASANNA
19th *July*, 1862. } SHINGHA.

Witness.
Sree Nobin Chunder Mukerji.
„ Kristo Das Pal.

COPIES OF PRIVATE LETTERS ADDRESSED TO THE BIOGRAPHER.

(1st Letter.)

CALCUTTA,
Dated 26th September, 1876.

MY DEAR SIR,

You are quite right. I was very busy of late, as I told you often I am a bad correspondent, being no master of my own time, and that I therefore beg of my friends to excuse me for my ipability to answer the notes as frequently as I could wish. But of this you may be assured that every line addressed to me commands my best attention.

Sidney Smith's allusion to "Kyme" you will find in his contributions to the *Edinburgh Review* on Indian Empire. I read it when I was in the College.

Thanks for your budget of news. Permit me to tell you that I can publish those items only that is not communicated to other papers. The *Patriot* always claims priority. Thanks for your kind wishes. Wishing you in return the compliments of the season and health and prosperity.

Yours sincerely,
(Sd.) KRISTO DAS PAL.

BABU RAM GOPAL SANYAL,
Krishnagar.

ANECDOTE.

(2nd Letter.)
108, BARANASHEE GHOSE'S STREET,
5th *July* 1876.

MY DEAR SIR,

I am not surprised to hear of the difficulties thrown in your way. This is the fate of all persons who have the temerity to write for the Press from the dark Mufussil. Those whose deeds are dark shun the light. I would, however, advise you to take care of yourself. Do not compromise your own interests in order to serve the Public. The circumstances of every man do not allow him to assert the right of a free man. I shall always be glad to hear from you and you may rest assured that your confidence will be never abused by me. At the same time take care of the traps which may be laid to catch you.

Yours sincerely,
(Sd.)   KRISTO DAS PAL.

BABU RAM GOPAL SANYAL.

ANECDOTES.

Babu Kristo Das Pal's visit to Ranaghat and Krishnaghar in the District of Nuddea.

It was in the year 1881 the Hon'ble Kristo Das Pal visited the above places. Neither pleasure nor curiosity was the motive of his personal visit to these places of historic renown. Krishnaghur is one of the ancient seats of Hindoo monarchy in Bengal, having obtained the name from the immortal Maharaja Krishna Chunder Roy Bahadur, who took a conspicuous part in the revolution which placed the Government of Bengal in the hands of the East India Company.

Ranaghat is no less famous, being the native village of that Great Incarnation of Charity, I mean the famous Kristo Panti of immortal fame. Occupied as Babu Kristo Das was with the various duties of a journalist and a public man, he had neither the time nor the inclination to go on a visit to villages in order to enjoy rural scenes. He was a man of stern reality and not given to pleasure-hunting. The greatest aim of his life was, to devote his whole time and energy to ameliorate the condition of his fellow countrymen, and in trying to achieve that end, he died a martyr, it might be said, to the cause of this great country. His popularity may be judged from the circumstances on account of which he was obliged to go to these places. A man named Deno Nath Goswain personated himself as a Deputy Collector to levy tax for the Afghan War from the people of Ranaghat and other adjoining places, under orders from the Government. Knowing that the name of the Hon'ble Kristo Das Pal would carry great weight with the people of Bengal, he gave out that the appointment had been procured for him by the Hon'ble Kristo Das from Lord Ripon himself, and he produced forged letters of appointment bearing the signatures and the initials of His Excellency the Marquis of Ripon, and his Private Secretary, Mr. Primrose.

The forgery was easily detected by the then Sub-divisional officer of Ranaghat, Babu Ram Charan Bose, and the culprit was brought to trial. In the course of this trial, Kristo Das was summoned as a witness in the Ranaghat Deputy Magistrate's Court. Kristo Das appeared before the Court, and denied having the least knowledge of the pseudo-Collector Denonath. He respectfully represented to the Court that as he was a very hard-worked and busy man, his presence could have been easily dispensed with, and when the Court replied that his evidence was considered material in the case, Kristo Das respectfully submitted, why was not the evidence of the Governor-General and his Private Secretary considered in the same light ? The Deputy Magistrate then facetiously asked, whether it was desirable that the Governor-General should be summoned, and Kristo Das smiled and said nothing. The elite of the native community of Ranaghat headed by the popular zemindar Babu Surendra Nath Pal Chowdhry, one of the grandsons of Kristo Panti gave him a cordial welcome. His cordial manners, suavity of temperament, and courtesy won the golden opinions of all the people assembled on that occasion, and made a deep impression on them.

Denonath was committed to the Sessions Court of Nuddea for trial and there, too, Kristo Das was unwilling to go for pressure of business. The leaders of the native community of Krishnaghar tried their best to bring him to Krishnaghar on this occasion and to shew their respect to him. He became the guest of the Government pleader, Babu Ram Chander Mukerjee, and there he came in contact with almost every man of importance in the town. It is related by Babu Ram Chander Mukerjee himself, that at a select dinner party in his house, Kristo Das astonished the assembled guests when he refused, following the time-honoured custom amongst the Hindus, to take anything before the Brahmans took their *gondoos*.

It is hardly necessary to add that Kristo Das won the respect of the Krishnaghur people. We shall finish this anecdote by relating another circumstance which concerns the writer himself. It will shew beyond doubt the large-mindedness of the Hon'ble Kristo Das Pal. During his short stay at Krishnaghur, Kristo Das did not forget to pay a visit to the poor family of the biographer who was then absent from home. It was purely a friendly visit, and this act of condescension on his part might be appreciated by those who know the worth of real friendship.

The following anecdote of his life is taken from the *Hindoo Patriot* of the 30th November, 1886 which contains an extract from the *Indian Spectator* of Bombay :—

"If any one deserved a faithful record after his death of what manner of man he was when living, it was Babu Kristo Das. The son of a commoner, Rajas and Princes and other elites of the land delighted to be seen in his company and to be reckoned amongst his friends. Not a measure was thought of or discussed in Council by Government, but the first question was to know what would Kristo Das say to it. There was not an European, official or non-official, but had recourse to the Babu in any case requiring consultation. Yet with such an enviable position, the Babu never lost his balance. Mr. Gladstone has reviewed Trevelyan's Life of Macaulay in the *Quarterly*, and in the course of the review he mentions that Macaulay, though courted by royalty and fawned on by the aristocracy, never thought of keeping an equipage of his own till after his return from India. The same was the case with Babu Kristo Das. Though moving in the highest circles, he was simple and inexpensive in his taste to the last, and was always seen going to the Council Chamber in Government House on meeting days in a common hackery or a hired palanquin. It is related of Dickens that on one occasion he received a £1,000 note from the famous Holloway with a request that the novelist would but introduce Holloway's name in one of his works. Dickens, without making fuss about the matter, quietly returned the money without any note or remark. A similar anecdote is related of Babu Kristo Das. On one occasion a grandee of the land, whose case was shortly to come on before Government, which involved the grant of a large amount of money, bespoke the Babu's advocacy of his cause in the *Hindoo Patriot* by sending him a large *douceur* in advance. The Babu, however, knew himself too well. He took one or two intimate friends into his confidence in regard to the circumstance, and then quietly sent back the money to the donor with the intimation that if his cause was just, the *Hindoo Patriot* would require no inducement for its advocacy. Well may Calcutta be proud of such a man, and well may the Bengalis preserve such a career in amber. But we have recourse again to the same question—What have our friends over the way done in this matter?

It may not be generally known on this side, that Kristo Das's immediate predecessor in the editorial chair of the *Hindoo Patriot* was a man of no ordinary mark. Hurish Chander Mukerjee enjoyed no ordinary reputation both amongst Natives and Europeans by the conduct of his paper. During the Mutinies, the *Patriot* in the Babu's hands, was more than a match for the combined strength of all the English papers of Bengal, and during the Indigo Rebellion, as it is called, the Babu piloted the cause of the *Jaquerre* in such a masterly way that he extorted respect even from his opponents. He too was cut off prematurely, and strange as it may appear, Calcutta owes the record of his life to a Bombay man. This life is contained in a book entitled *Lights and Shades* of the East. We may also add that towards the subscription which was got up in honour of the deceased, Bombay sent its quota—the Bombay subscription being promoted by Mr. Sorabjee Shapurjee Bengali. A reading room known as Hurish Reading Room, attached to the office of the British Indian Association, is the form of the Babu to the present generation."

SPECIMEN OF BABU HURISH CHANDER MUKERJEE'S WRITINGS IN 1857.

THE HINDOO PATRIOT.
Thursday, December 31st, 1857.

In making these extracts from the writings of this renowned Journalist, we may be permitted to say that the old files of the *Hindoo Patriot* before the year 1857 cannot be found neither in the rooms of the British Indian Association nor in the Metcalf Hall, and we are therefore, so far as our space permits, content with transcribing the following articles from his writings in 1857 and 1858.

"The year 1857 will form the date of an era unsurpassed in importance by any in the history of mankind. For us who are living in the midst of those scenes which have stampt this epochal character on the year, it is impossible to realize in its fullest measure the interest that will attach to it in the eyes of posterity. Our minds are too full of the incidents of the rebellion—of this siege and that massacre, the battle, the retreat, the ambuscade, mutinies, treacheries and treasons—they are far too agitated,—to receive a fair image of the present. The rebellion came upon us with a shock for which no class of the community was prepared. It has taken by surprise the country—not excepting the vast body of the rebels themselves. For eight long months it has ravaged the land in its length and breadth, spreading crime and misery of every hue and form. And when now its strength has been broken and its end has made itself visible, it bids fair to leave the nation a legacy of prolonged and yet unknown troubles."

"The dawn of the year 1857 disclosed to us prospects than which more hopeful could not be conceived in the destiny of a people. The country was tranquil at home and at peace abroad. The reckless spirit of territorial aggrandisement which absorbed the energies of Government for the previous eight years had passed away. The condition of the people, the great social interests of the nation had become an object of earnest attention. A healthy political spirit characterised the proceedings of the intelligent classes of the community, who were prepared and disposed to support the views of an enlightened legislature. Grand schemes of law and social reform propounded by men of the greatest ability, were in agitation. Education, public works, and material improvements were receiving a stronger impulse than ever urged them forward. The public finances were slowly recovering from the exhaustion into which they had fallen. Plans of retrenchment had been set on foot with the best chances of success. Never did the country enter upon a new year with brighter hopes or in better spirits."

"But the calculations of man are as nought in the course of Providence. We shall not presume to enter into speculations as to the causes of the mutinies. It is too early to determine how the Sepoy mind became so strongly embued with the idea that the Government was resolved to destroy their religion, and that they were strong enough by themselves to wrest India from the hands of the British. These causes would extend over a number of years, and their examination will be the business of history, not journalism. Nor shall we enter into a narrative of events, the memory of which is so terribly fresh in the minds of our readers. We may be content with noting what effect these events have had upon national progress during the year."

"First of all we have suffered in character from the effect of these mutinies. Despite multitudinous traducers, the national character of the Hindoos stood high in the eyes of the world. If we were described as superstitious, we were allowed to be an intellectual people. Against our want of patriotic and military order, a whole host of virtues was allowed to be more than a set-off. We have always suffered, history could produce no instance of our having inflicted suffering. If an account were cast up between us and the rest of the world, it would be found that the balance of benefits would be largely in our favour. There was much in our annals, institutions and literature which interested the scholar and the statesman alike; and made cultivated men in general view our nation with eyes of really affectionate regard. For the time, every sentiment of goodwill and respect that foreigners entertained for us is in a state of annihilation. The atrocities which have followed in the wake of the mutinies have been truly described as unspeakable. They have been charged most untruly and unjustly to the whole nation. We shall not deny the responsibility of the mutineers for every act of outrage which in the disorganization caused by their mutiny became possible of commission. But we deny that the moral character of the nation is to be estimated by the acts of the felonry of the country—the refuse, the dregs, the unhung scoundralism of the population. For the time this fact, so probable, so vraisemblant (?), is indignantly ignored; and we are charged with, besides an unlimited capacity for crime, having deceived the world for three thousand years by concealing from it that capacity."

"Along with the forfeiture of the good opinion of the civilized world, we have incurred another loss, if not equally great, more closely affecting our interests. For the time, the estrangement between the native races and the mass of the English people has become complete. We are objects not merely of suspicion; we have become objects of the bitterest hostility. Our British fellow-subjects firmly believe that we have embarked in a contest, the aim of which is their extermination. Extravagant as this belief is, it is too momentous in its consequences to be ridiculed. With their aid, we have secured many substantial benefits."

. "The time had just come when by more intimately commingling our interests with theirs, we were about winning many more. The commencement of the year saw our countrymen in hot contest with their British fellow-subjects for the acquisition of equal laws and equal rights. There was some bitterness in the contest, but there were the very best chances of success in our favour. The object once gained, the quarrel would have speedily faded from memory, and a community of interest would have engendered feelings that would have completely washed away the bitterness and soothed the antagonism of race. The mutinies have made coalition for a time impossible, and reconciliation a thing of distant hope."

"Our second great loss has been in the item of civilization. For a time, and that we fear no short a time, our path of social progress is completely barred. We cannot mend a barbarous, or a cruel, or an irrational custom, however large the majority anxious to do it, if the reform be one to need the aid of the law. The Widows' Marriage Act is an instance to prove the advanced position which the legislature had taken in respect to social matters. A law to restrain polygamy was on the tapis, and merely awaited a few formalities to have effective penal force throughout the country. Other abominations live which it were unpatriotic to expose to the gaze of idle curiosity. All these have gained a long lease of existence. All hopes of their extirpation lie for the time dashed to the ground. The legislature stands committed to a policy of inaction so far as regards them. It may give us good courts of justice, unexceptionable judicial procedure, and well-framed systems of taxation; but to draw out and destroy evils that are eating into the very core of social morals and happiness, our legislators have become—owing to the mutinies alone—utterly powerless."

"The extent of purely political loss that the mutinies will have inflicted upon the country yet remains to be estimated. Those aspirations after equality with the most favoured of the sovereign's subjects which so justifiably animated our political efforts, now seem vain and extravagant. The authorities themselves have given way to the pressure of the times, and succumbed to influences which are yet to attain their fullest development. The Directors have already countermanded the enactment of a law sanctioned by the approval of the greatest jurists and statesmen of the age, that should place the Briton and the Bengali upon the same footing in the eye of the law. That is but a sample of what possibly may yet be in store for us. It may yet be our lot to be trampled upon, to be thrown into the lowest stage of political existence that a conquered nation can be held down to, to be made to hew wood and draw water for conquerors who shall be our oppressors, to expiate in one long noviciate of serfdom sins not our own. These are gloomy forebodings, but the most sanguine, when he marks the temper of the times, cannot help now and then giving way to them."

"All material improvement is for the present at a halt. Our Railways instead of progressing have been partially destroyed. The electric telegraph which this time last year flashed messages across a continent, now lies mangled and torn. Irrigation and roads, works of utility and of ornament, schemes intended to succour and raise famished millions, have all been abandoned in the struggle for self-preservation. The heavy loss of life and property, and the heavier loss which insecurity and terrorism may yet occasion, remain to be counted. Computation is baffled in the attempt to determine the amount of physical suffering and sacrifices that the rebellion will have cost the natives of India. The list might be prolonged had the need been. But the painful task has become superfluous owing to the very universality of the suffering which prevails. There is not one among the inhabitants of this continent who, if not labouring under the mania of insurrection, does not feel and deplore in body, mind or estate its consequences. Generations of our countrymen will yet have to bear a share of the same sufferings. From contemplations like these we are driven for consolation to the immutable laws of Providence. The man of true historic faith sees in every event a stepping-stone for society to advance by in the path of progress. All is for the best. The Indian rebellion, with all its horrors, cannot be exempt from the operation of the historic law. And the year 1857, commemorated in characters of blood and fire, is probably destined to usher in an era of unexampled progress and happiness for a tenth of the human race."

SPECIMEN OF BABU HURISH CHANDER MUKERJEE'S WRITINGS IN 1860.

RELATIONS BETWEEN INDIGO PLANTERS AND RYOTS.

HINDOO PATRIOT.
February 4th, 1860.

The well-known Calcutta Barrister Mano Mohun Ghose, Esq. has pointed out this article written by Babu Hurish Chander during the Indigo Crisis of 1860 :—

"*Anarchy in Bengal.*—They speak what is literally a truth who speak of the prevalence of anarchy in some of the districts of Bengal. It is anarchy when a few men, by the mere force of the strong arm lord it over millions, and bar them from the benefits of government. The external show of courts, policemen, and officials, is a mockery in regions where the oppressed man cannot approach the law but by permission of his oppressor. It is anarchy there where lattialism is an institution for the maintenance of which its patrons openly contend with the legislature—where the iron will, the brave heart, and brute force will ensure their possessor complete supremacy.

And why should it be so? These districts, the seat of this anarchy, are within eyesight of a Government the strongest in Asia. The people are a race who require the least amount of government to keep their society together. It is a country of old traditions, which has known regular laws and courts of justice for narly a century. One single tax of four millions is borne by the people themselves to the public exchequer with a punctuality not observed by the seasons. Religion reigns in the land with more than ordinary force. And yet there is anarchy in Bengal.

The phenomenon is easily explicable. No branch of the internal administration of Bengal is so inefficient as the police and penal judicature. The ordinary magistracy has always been found incapable of coping with crimes of any magnitude. Whenever a form of great crime has to be put down, a special organization becomes needed. Weak in numerical strength, the magistracy is weaker in action. The discreditably low aim which the District Magistrates propose to themselves is pursued with a total lack of energy and vigour. The District Magistrate is satisfied if his superiors do not report him worse than his predecessor. He is more than satisfied if he keeps his district in no worse order than it was when he stepped into his office. The hard task of maintaining the very existence of peace is postponed to the less exacting duty of superintending roads and ferries, and tampering with the prospects of subordinates. Wanting confidence in himself, and perhaps in his official superiors too, he dares not grapple with the larger evils, or provoke the enmity of a powerful wrong-doer. The sufferings of a black man can never be an object of anything but occasional pity to a true son of Japhet. But the white Magistrate placed over a population of black men is so habituated, to sights of suffering and oppression, that they do not excite in his breast even that fashionable little sentiment. Genuine callousness of heart would pass for judicial impartiality, and indolence shelters itself under the guise of a constitutional respect for the law.

But the Magistrate, though the chief custodian of the peace in his own district, is after all, it may be said, a responsible officer. He is but a subordinate in a hierarchy of many grades. There is his diocesan, the Commissioner of the Division. What does he do? It is his duty to see that the Magistrate performs his duty. To that end he moves from station to station, the doing which he calls his tour of inspection. Inspect he often does, as the shelves of the fouzdaree record-room and the roads of the cutcherry compound at seasons abundantly testify. Control the Magistrate he does; or why does every darogah, mohurrir, jemadar, or burkundauz, who has been fined, suspended, or dismissed, feel that he does himself injustice until he has appealed to the Commissioner? No Commissioner of Division, however, feels it necessary to enquire into the state of the more vital matters affecting the well-being of his district. It is no business of his to goad the indolent, instruct the inexperienced, or to check the aberrations of the corrupt. With his subordinates he shares the sweet calm of a disposition not to be ruffled by sights of suffering and oppression.

The Commissioner again is but a suffragan. There is his metropolitan, the Government of Bengal. The Government of Bengal was a few years ago composed of the leisure moments of a statesman whose proper duties occupied him twelve hours a day, and of the weaknesses of a Secretary who would be outcasted if he wrote a strong letter of censure of his own accord. Since the conversion of the Government of Bengal into an entity, it has indeed made itself individually felt. The first incarnate Government of Bengal was a man whose knowledge of the country was unbounded. High hopes were entertained of him. His first act raised those hopes higher than ever. He recorded his opinion in sententious terms, that everywhere the Strong oppressed the Weak. The opinion—a truism—had all the charms of a discovery when it proceeded from Mr. Halliday's mouth; for it was universally believed that the truism was soon to be converted, in a great measure at least, into a myth in the dominions of the Government of Bengal. People expectantly waited for the remedy. That was soon proposed. It was to destroy the Strong—to leave none but the Weak. The strong proved too strong for the destroyer. It was not the idiosyncrasy of the vigorous minute-writer to take action after the publication of his minute. The Strong everywhere continued to oppress the Weak.

With one branch of the Strong family the first Government of Bengal cultivated relation which affected the condition of the Weak very materially. The first Government of Bengal was considerably in advance of the rest of mankind in his views of policy; and the development of the resources of the country was an extremely favoured object of his political sympathies. Therefore, and for another reason,' namely, that the said Government was very pardonably ambitious of a British fame, he patronized with all his might the branch of the strong family which made indigo and coal. He knew how indigo and coal were made. But he tolerated all, and discouraged every attempt of everybody that interfered with the production of indigo and coal.

Mr. Halliday's successor has been but a few months in the office. That he has already grown so popular is as much due to the fact of his being Mr. Halliday's successor as to the unqualified respect entertained for his character, and the boundless confidence felt in his impartiality and love of justice. This last is an advantage which will stand him in good stead whenever his acts offend a class or injure a pampered interest. He has already taken the first step towards the restoration of law and order in the seats of anarchy. There is no doubt that it will not be the last. But we doubt whether even Mr. Grant will be able to cow his subordinates to co-operate with him in the great task. They are not accustomed to believe that anarchy needs to be removed, whilst the "station" is safe and the revenues are paid in. They have no idea that the anarchy can be removed, or any good will come out of anything being substituted for it. They object to the novelty and the troublesomeness of the task sought to be imposed upon them. Some of quicker instincts see political danger in the entire suppression of anarchy in the land. Others believe that the development of the resources will cease. All will vote Mr. Grant a bore.

The question has become a serious one. The ryots, if they have not learnt that Mr. Grant has forbidden the cultivation of indigo, have learnt that Mr. Halliday is no longer Governor. Mr. Tottenham's magistracy of a few weeks has given them the idea that justice is not always unattainable. A spirit, such as we never in our weakest moments anticipated, has made its appearance in the indigo-growing districts. The poor fellows may in the end succumb. But between the date and this there will occur a series of social collisions which will simply disgrace established authority. We supplicate our rulers to ward off these occurrences."

SPECIMEN OF BABU KRISTO DAS'S WRITINGS IN 1858.

THE HINDOO PATRIOT.
January 21st, 1858.

THE LATE BABU RUSSICK KRISHNA MULLICK.

For want of space we make the following extract from his contributions to the *Hindoo Patriot* in 1858. Besides this Kristo Das wrote the review of the novel called *Alalghurer Dulal* by the late Babu Peary Chand Mitra and several other articles :—

" Something more than a formal paragraph notice is due to the memory of the man whose life was the history of the early struggle which marked native progress in the beginning, and the leading fact of whose existence was to sustain the character his intelligence, energy and courage obtained for him. Babu Russick Krishna Mullick lived in the commencement of an intellectual and moral revolution, yet in course of completion, and was himself a brave leader in it. Perhaps Bengal had then received a greater shock than whole India has met with in this gigantic revolt of the Sepoys. Rammohan Roy was teaching pure lessons of Holiness and God, and throwing doubts and questions upon the veracity and purity of the doctrines of the Shasters and Poorans. The war between Brahminism and Brahmoism, between principle and prejudice, between liberty and despotism, between prescription and progress, then commenced. English education was sending forth its triumphs in a noble set of young Bengalees, with enlightened ideas of society and of civilization, and with courage and energy to follow and disseminate them. David Hare was memorializing his life by a career of enlightened zeal and usefulness inducing the children of our fathers to taste the fruits of knowledge, and to receive light wherewith to dispel the darkness which enveloped their country. Dr. Duff, with his youthful buoyancy and young missionary enthusiasm, had then newly commenced to inveigh against the idolatry of the people and to preach the merits and transcendancies of Christianity. Such was the morning of the era, the noon of which we now dimly see. Although the lamented deceased was not the only person who seconded the spirit of the time, he was one of those who placed themselves in advance of the general run of their countrymen by shewing a bold front to all cold threats and disheartening attacks. Those who remember the time which saw this early contest of civilization with deep-rooted prejudice and inexorable antagonism of feeling in the same race, will be at no difficulty to imagine that Babu Russick Krishna Mullick was thrown upon his own resources by his family which was then in a highly prosperous condition for pursuing knowledge with an unflagging perseverance, and for framing the conduct of his life after the principles which English authors inculcated. But his zeal was unconquerable; his courage indomitable. With a rich and fertile mind, replenished with the sentiments of the best English authors, and disciplined to an admirable training he was a pride to the old Hindu College. He early attracted the notice of Dr. Wilson, and was marked out by Sir Edward Ryan as one far above the average of Bengali scholars. His ready elocution won for him deserved applause at the Academical Society, the first Native Club, patronized at the time by highly distinguished public servants and the most eminent men of education of the day. His desire to diffuse the blessings of education led him along with other friends to start the *Guananeshun*, an Anglo-Bengali Journal, through the medium of which the soundest maxims of morals and the most useful lessons of life were promulgated. He was one of the few literary enthusiasts who formed the circle of which H. V. Derozio and Dr. Adams were the centre. The age was indeed a golden age. Education was a new gift, and was accordingly valued at even more than its proper worth, and Lord William Bentinck even did not feel it derogatory to his dignity as Governor-General of India to associate with an educated native of however humble origin. There was then less of that mean pride, and petty jealousy which form so disagreeable a feature in the character of nine-tenths of both the official and non-official classes of the European community in this country. Babu Russick Krishna Mullick began life as a teacher in Mr. Hare's school and closed it with the highest honours which an Uncovenanted servant could obtain. Although the best part of his life was spent in the dark arena of the mofussil, he used seldom to omit any opportunity during his visits to Calcutta to lend his aid and energy to the cause of the class of which he was truly a representative man. His opinions on public men and measures, were such as every enlightened man would respect. He rarely appeared before the public in the capacity of a speaker, but when he did, his admirable fluency and pure English used to carry the minds of the audience. But he was extremely modest in the estimate of his own worth, and he never aspired to the position of one of the public characters of Bengal. The goodness of his heart may be appreciated by the fact that he bequeathed at the time of his death a sum of five thousand rupees to the District Charitable Society. In him we have lost one of the links which connect the days of Rammohan Roy and David Hare with ours. We are told he has left a manuscript book containing thoughts of Religion, and we hope his friends will in justice to the memory of the author, publish it. Other contributions from his pen to the Indian Press, though displaying to no small advantage the talent and intellectual attainments of the writer do not, we think, possess a durable interest. We, however, deeply deplore his death which is a personal loss to us and to a large circle of friends. Peace be to his memory!"

The above article has been shewn to us by Babu Shumbhoo Chander Mukerjee, the Editor of the *Reis and Ryut*.

FINIS.

www.ingramcontent.com/pod-product-compliance
Lightning Source LLC
Chambersburg PA
CBHW020905230426
43666CB00008B/1320